identity
A SOUL JOURNEY

a GLAM resource | by Brooke Lee

Copyright © 2016 by Brooke Lee
All Rights Reserved

Cover Design: Aly Allen
Interior Design: Aly Allen
Font Used with Permission: Frente H1, designed by studio Frente (frente.cc)

This book was self-published by Brooke Lee. No part of this book may be reproduced in any form by any means without the express permission of the author. This includes reprints, excerpts, photocopying, recording, or any future means of reproducing text.

If you would like to do any of the above, please seek permission first by contacting us at glaminformation@gmail.com.

Published in the United States of America

First Printing, 2016

ISBN 978-0-692-66489-6

www.godlovesallofme.org

A LETTER FROM ME TO YOU

H E L L O Lovely!

My name is Brooke. I truthfully wish I could be meeting you face to face right now. There are few things I love more than sitting across the table from a lovely woman doing real- talk. Although I can't do that with each of you, I thought it was important to write a letter to you, giving you a little background on who I am.

I grew up in Las Vegas, Nev. I had the same longings you probably had or have growing up; I wanted to be liked, accepted and loved and I wanted to fit in. I still have those longings.

Growing up, I always saw my weight as an issue. I felt less than other girls because of my weight, and I definitely based my worth and value mostly in my appearance. Sometimes I still do this.

I suffered through an eating and exercise disorder from late high school into early college. I'm still healing from that.

I've made lots of mistakes. I used to try and cover them up or blame someone else; now I try to embrace them and learn from them. I'm a recovering perfectionist and control-freak, learning grace and surrender. The latter is awesome, but sometimes I still choose the former.

I lost my sister tragically in 2011 to drug addiction. I share this part of my journey with you because I want you to know that I understand gut-wrenching pain and loss. My heart still writhes in pain from time to time. My heart also beats with more joy and passion than ever before. Grief has taught me the paradox of joy and pain existing simultaneously. This side of Heaven, I won't fully understand my sister's death, and I'm okay with that. What I do understand is that God has the amazing ability to bring good from every terrible experience. And He's done just that.

I love God. Oh, do I love Him. It's a broken, messy, sometimes confusing kind of love, but it's real. I don't always do what He desires for me, and we have communication errors from time to time. Yet, even still, He is my everything. One moment with Him surpasses anything I have ever experienced. I really mean that.

I used to think religious ways were God's requirements of us—cruel and mean and His attempt at preventing us from having fun. I also thought they were ways to earn our spot in heaven. I've since learned that God gives us guidelines as a gift, knowing that they will lead us to the most joy and satisfaction while here on this earth. Oh and I've also learned that our spot in heaven is all about whether or not we accept Jesus. Really, it's that simple.

I crave authenticity. I hate small talk.

I'm an introvert. Most people think I'm an extrovert. I avoid large group gatherings and parties like the plague, not because I don't love people, it's actually the opposite. I love people so much that I want to do deep, real-talk and it's hard to do that at large group gatherings.

I have a passion for women. I love women. I've spent lots of years comparing to and competing with women, and I don't like it. I want us all to be on the same team, cheering each other on, helping each other fight and sharpening each other to be the women God created us to be. But, there's junk that gets in the way of us doing that. I want to help us clear out that junk.

I strive for balance in my life, though I don't always reach it. I'm married to an incredible, imperfect, God-loving man. He is one of the sweetest gifts I have received from God.

More than most things in my life, I really care about this workbook. I want it to be useful. I want it to help you the way it is helping me. And, I want you to experience the goodness of God through it. I have prayed and prayed and asked others to pray that God would use this workbook to change your life. I believe God has heard our prayers and plans on doing just that.

It's nice to meet you, my dear!

Brooke :)

CONTENTS

INTRODUCTION: WHY THIS WORKBOOK MATTERS	5
VIDEO TEACHING LINKS & INFORMATION	9
TO DO BEFORE YOU BEGIN	10
CHAPTER 1: PREPARING FOR THE JOURNEY	11
Day 1: The Structure & How to Navigate	14
Day 2: This is a Soul-Journey, Not a Bible Study	17
Day 3: Reminders	21
Day 4: Capturing Your Story	23
Day 5: Practicing Your Story	25
CHAPTER 2: UNCOVERING MY IDENTITY	26
Day 1: Characteristics, Roles & Dreams	30
Day 2: Worth & Value	35
Day 3: Childhood	39
Day 4: Events, Happenings, & Circumstances	43
Day 5: Faith & God	46
CHAPTER 3: GOD-GIVEN IDENTITY	49
Day 1: The Foundation of the God-Given Identity	53
Day 2: Unique Qualities & Characteristics	57
Day 3: Spiritual Gifts	61
Day 4: Childhood & Experiences	63
Day 5: Transformation & Purpose	65
CHAPTER 4: SELF-CREATED IDENTITY	71
Day 1: The Foundation of the Self-Created Identity	75
Day 2: Qualities & Characteristics	77
Day 3: Passions, Skills & Interests	80
Day 4: Childhood & Experiences	82
Day 5: Pursuing Perfection Cause & Effect	85
CHAPTER 5: PROCESSING MY IDENTITY	89
Day 1: Listening for God	93
Day 2: Characteristics, Roles & Dreams	96
Day 3: Personal Value & Faith	101
Day 4: Childhood	104
Day 5: Events, Experiences, & Circumstances	106

CHAPTER 6: SURRENDER — 110

Day 1: Preparing to Surrender — 116
Day 2: Processing Surrender — 118
Day 3: Repentance, Forgiveness, & Healing — 120
Day 4: Forgiveness of Self — 125
Day 5: Decision — 127

CHAPTER 7: APPLY & PRACTICE THE GOD-GIVEN IDENTITY — 128

Day 1: Qualities, Characteristics, Dreams & Passions — 133
Day 2: Personal Value — 137
Day 3: Spiritual Gifts, Strengths, & Talents — 142
Day 4: Faith & God — 144
Day 5: Experiences, Roles & Childhood — 145

CONCLUSION: WHAT NOW? — 150

Conclusion — 151
Resources — 153
Thank You — 154
Receiving Christ — 156
The GLAM Ministry — 158

introduction

WHY THIS WORKBOOK MATTERS

Who are you? What makes you, you? What is your identity?

These questions may cause you to fill up with anxiety, or confidently rattle off a list of characteristics, roles and/or titles.

Either way, whether you have an answer or not, every person identifies themselves somehow. There is some makeup of who you know yourself to be that separates you from anyone else. There are characteristics, feelings, experiences and interests you find definition in, which in turn results in your identity.

Your identity is what defines you.

Not only does your identity define you, it also directs you and the course of your life. I like to think of identity as a sort of steering mechanism for our lives.

Who you are, or rather, who you know yourself to be, dictates your choices, relationships and pursuits.

Think about it: When faced with a decision for which job to take, who to date and/or marry, which people to call friends and what opportunities to pursue, it is your identity and who you know yourself to be that directs your steps.

Those directions may come by way of feeling (we feel more drawn to a certain opportunity) or by way of head-knowledge (we know in our heads that an opportunity is in line with who we are). This is how we make decisions, and right there, smack dab in the middle of all that decision making, is the steering wheel of identity.

Our identity defines us and directs us.

From those directions in life come either satisfaction or dissatisfaction, contentment or discontentment, fulfillment or the lack thereof, joy or depression, freedom or bondage.

In a nutshell, identity has the power to steer our life down paths of abundance or paths of disappointment.

I'd say the stakes are high when it comes to our identity.

WHAT WE ALL WANT

Whether you believe in God or not, whether you've prayed "the prayer" or have no idea what "the prayer" is, whether you are on the fence or running, whether you are fully committed or completely skeptical, I'm going to make a wild guess that you care about your life. I'm also going to guess that you want to live a life that is worth living.

Almost every human being has a desire to live a life that matters. While it's true that there are a number of human beings who have given up on that desire, it doesn't negate the fact that the desire is there...probably just buried deep down inside.

Most, if not all of us, are seeking the kind of life that bursts with joy, makes our heart feel warm and full, feels exhilarating, spills over with purpose, gives us the experience of love and belonging and is littered with passion.

We want a life that is living and breathing.

If this is true, that most human beings have this desire, then why is it that there are so many of us slumping through an unfulfilled, discontent, and joyless life...and doing so all in secret?

We are consumed with the dishes piling high in the sink, our never ending to-do lists, the carpooling, the corporate ladder climbing, the image we see in the mirror or the number on the scale, the constant scum-ring around our bathtubs and the seemingly endless pursuit of being good-enough, all the while wondering, "surely, there is more to life than this."

It seems at times that our lives are riddled with brokenness, busyness and struggle, rather than joy, peace, passion and contentment.

What is the disconnect? What causes the schism between the life we want to be living and the life we are actually living?

I believe that disconnect has almost everything to do with identity -- who we know ourselves to be and which identity we are living life out of.

THIS WORKBOOK

This workbook is primarily focused on identity. If it's true that our identity has the power to lead our lives toward abundance or deprivation, I think it's safe to say that exploring identity is well worth our time.

I would like to make a quick disclaimer for those of you who have heard a plethora of sermons on identity, read countless books on the topic or have heard the phrase "find your identity in Christ" one too many times. I see you, I get you, and there is something in these pages for you.

Often times, at least for me, I hear wonderful truths about identity, but time after time they remain an idea, rather than something practical I can apply to my life.

The writing of this workbook has come from a burning desire to give us practical ways of "finding our identity in Christ." Here's what you'll find in the pages that follow:

In the first section, you will prepare for the journey ahead. You will be asked questions about why you decided to do this workbook and what you are hoping to get out of it. It will sort of be like packing for a trip.

The second chapter is all about uncovering the life you are living now and who you know yourself to be today. You'll answer several pages of questions to help you uncover this. Think of it like taking inventory. Let's check under the hood and see what's there.

Once you've uncovered your starting place, you'll learn about two different options you can choose from when it comes to your identity: a God-given identity or a self- created identity. Chapters three and four will address questions like: How do these types of identities form? Are we unique and do our unique qualities matter to God? Which qualities were formed within us and which were developed out of an experience? Are self-created identities completely false?

The fifth chapter will allow you time to process through these two different types of identity as they relate to you. There will be a series of questions to help guide you through this processing stage. You'll reflect back on the answers you gave in the second chapter and discover how those answers fit into the different types of identity revealed in chapters three and four. You will be given the opportunity to label areas of your life that are self-created and God-given, as well as identify the struggles that get in the way of you living out of your God-given identity.

If I have learned anything in my walk with God, it is that any change I want to make in my life comes first by way of surrender. Chapter six will suggest a number of ways for you to surrender those areas of your life where you want to see change. Don't worry; I'll also unpack what "surrender" really means. It's a church-y word that gets thrown around a lot without any explanation, so we'll do our best to understand it. This chapter will also offer a step-by-step process for how to surrender, ending with an opportunity to practice surrender at your group gathering.

You will conclude this workbook by taking action. This is where that practical application comes into play. There will be pages of practices for you to look through and choose from. Think of it like shopping. You'll browse through lists of practices and choose the ones that jump out to you. Then, you'll try them out, process them and reflect on what worked and didn't work.

THE JOURNEY

It's important as you begin that you see this workbook (and your life) as a journey. Understanding and applying your identity is not a mountain-top summit or something to conquer. In fact, you probably won't have complete clarity on your identity by the time you finish this workbook, nor will your life be free of struggle. These things will most likely be something you pursue and grow in for the rest of your life.

I apologize if I just busted your bubble, or worse, if I've led you to want to abandon this workbook for the lack of a mountain-top summit. Before any of you do, just listen to why I think you should journey on.

What has happened in our culture is that we've been enticed over and over again by all of these quick and easy step-by-step plans to change our life: Five Ways to the New You. Seven Steps to Success. Three Secrets to Changing Your Life.

The truth is, these step by step plans offer quick, temporary fixes, rather than deep, lasting life-change. We know this is true because most of us have gone through one or more of these processes only to come up empty. It may have been quick, but it sure as heck didn't offer any lasting change. This is nothing to feel bad about. The thought of my life changing in just a few simple steps seems wonderful. Romantic, even. But we all know that lasting change from these quick, step-by-step processes remains a fantasy, not reality.

Every true and lasting change that I can think of has taken place over time. And it definitely didn't come from six easy, chronological steps.

True and lasting change is a blend of backwards and forwards, risks and complacency, failures and successes, attempts, bravery, vulnerability, humility, stamina, strength and perseverance, all laid out over time.

True and lasting change is a journey.

It will help if you view this workbook as part of that journey or the framework of that journey.

What I do hope, once you have finished this workbook, is that you will have a clear understanding of a self-created identity and a God-given identity. I also hope that you will have experienced God and his freedom, even if it's in the tiniest of ways. Finally, I hope that you will feel equipped with tools that you can continue to use and apply to your journey of transforming identity.

So, with that being said, I am excited to journey with you. I'm excited for you to journey with other women. And most of all, I'm excited for the transformation that awaits you amidst your journey.

The really good stuff isn't found at the end, my dear; it's found in the steps you take to get there.

So, let's get stepping.

VIDEO TEACHING LINKS & INFORMATION

Every chapter has a video teaching that your group will watch together before you begin the next chapter. You can find these video teachings online by following the simple steps below.

TO ACCESS THE VIDEO TEACHINGS:

1. Go to vimeo.com/ondemand/glamidentity
2. Find the video that is titled according to your upcoming week. For example, for the first week you will look for "Chapter 1, Preparing for the Journey." For the second week you will look for "Chapter 2, Uncovering My identity," and so on and so forth.
3. Each video is available for purchase. You can either purchase each chapter's video individually, or purchase all seven video sessions at once.

WE RECOMMEND WATCHING THE TEACHINGS IN A FEW WAYS:

1. On a computer with access to the internet
2. Through your television from a streaming device (such as AppleTV)

A PERSONAL REQUEST

I have done everything I can to keep the cost of these videos as low as possible to honor you. I just want to ask for your respect and honor back by not sharing these videos for free. Every penny from these videos goes back into our GLAM Ministries fund, which is used to reach women. So, when you purchase it, watch it with your group and please don't pass it along to other groups. I would be so grateful.

TO DO BEFORE YOU BEGIN

Complete this page at your first gathering before watching the first video teaching.

EXCHANGE CONTACT INFORMATION

As you go throughout this workbook, reach out to other group members. Invite a woman from your group out for coffee. Text or call each other during the week just to check in and see how things are going. There will be reminders throughout the workbook to connect with the women in your group. Just look for the boxes that say "DO THIS."

Pass your book to each person in your group and have them write their phone number and email below.

MAKE A GROUP COMMITMENT

Make a promise to God, to yourself and to the other person or people in your group that you will stick this out to the end and that you will make this group a priority. Things may get hard, awkward, uncomfortable...don't quit when these things hit! It's important to remember that there is also great love, freedom, healing and transformation in store if you can stick it out to the end. Also, decide if there are any other guidelines (for example: what is shared in the group stays in the group, no posting on social media, cell phones put away) that your group wants to follow and write out your promise, in your own words, here:

CHAPTER 1
Preparing for the Journey

notes

CHAPTER 1 VIDEO SESSION

Our identity does two things:
- it defines us
- it directs us

Back in the day names were given because they signified meaning

New names were given all throughout the Bible:
Abram to Abraham (Genesis 17:1-5)
Sarai to Sarah (Genesis 17:15-16)
Jacob to Israel (Genesis 32:24-28)

John 1:42
"Jesus looked at him and said, 'You are Simon, son of John. You will be called Cephas,' which when translated is Peter."

Cephas (Aramaic) = Petros (Greek) = Rock or Bedrock (English)

Peter's new name meant bedrock. Peter was the bedrock on which the early church was built, a strong pillar that held up the early church.

PERSONAL NOTES:

introduction
PREPARING FOR THE JOURNEY

Trips, vacations, and journeys require preparation. Whether it's booking hotel rooms, or simply planning the dates in which you will be away, they each require some amount of forethought and planning before the actual journey begins.

I remember back to my first ever solo journey: college. Bed, Bath & Beyond became my official preparation headquarters. My mom wanted to make sure I was prepared with everything I needed for my new, yet temporary home; bedding, bathroom toiletries, laundry hamper, hangers, and such. Along with preparing for my new home, I also needed to prepare for school, so I did things like attended freshman orientation, connected with my roommate before I arrived, and decided what classes I would take.

Even the simplest of journeys, such as a trip to the grocery store, requires some level of preparation. I need to make sure I have money in my account to buy the groceries, gas in my car to get me there, and an idea of what food I will buy.

Preparation is essential to every journey and it's meant for our benefit. Our preparation is what determines how successful, fruitful, and enjoyable our journey will be. This chapter is all about preparing you for the journey that is ahead of you in this workbook. There are some things you need to know, formatting that you should be aware of, and some things you need to do before you begin. This chapter of preparation is meant to set you up for success; to prepare you for a fruitful and enjoyable journey ahead.

Before you jump in, I want you to take a minute and talk with God. There will be a simple prayer at the end of each chapter introduction to help remind us who our guide is for the journey. With that being said, will you pray with me?

PRAYER

God, I don't want to just go through these pages mindlessly.
I want to truly prepare for the journey you are going to lead me on.
Will you help prepare me? Will you open up my heart, mind, and soul to you?
Help me to see the things that are in the way of journeying with you.
Break down walls that I've built up within me. I'm ready! Amen.

day one

THE STRUCTURE & HOW TO NAVIGATE

This workbook is broken up into a seven-chapter journey on identity:

Ch. 1 - Preparing for the Journey
Ch. 2 - Uncovering My Identity
Ch. 3 - Truth: God-Given Identity
Ch. 4 - Truth: Self-Created Identity
Ch. 5 - Processing My Identity
Ch. 6 - Surrender
Ch. 7 - Apply & Practice the God-Given Identity

EACH CHAPTER

Each week you will go through a different chapter of the workbook. The chapters are divided into 5 days of content. When you begin a new chapter, the plan is for you to read the introduction, and fill out all of the pages for day one. The next day, fill out all of the pages for day two, and so on and so forth.

DISCUSSION TIME

Before starting the next chapter, you will come together for your weekly gathering to discuss the chapter you worked through the week before.

Can we have a little heart-to-heart chat about discussion real quick? I'm guessing that some of you feel a bit apprehensive when it comes to discussion. Perhaps it causes you feelings of awkwardness, fear, or maybe you are making, or have already made, the mental decision that you will just be sharing the surface-level stuff, rather than the real-life stuff. I get it. I've held back from sharing because I thought others would think less of me. I've felt the pangs of judgment, and the lack of support, and the let down of no one following up with me after I've shared. I've felt the frustration of someone trying to fix me, when all I really wanted was for someone to listen. I've boiled with anger at someone's inappropriate response. Maybe you've felt some of these things, too?

Although these feelings are valid, they aren't reason enough to avoid discussion.

Discussion will be messy at times; we are imperfect people. We won't always do the right thing or say the right thing. But, discussion has the potential to be one of the most healing things you and I will ever experience.

Chapter 1 | Preparing for the Journey

Do you want to know how that healing and powerful discussion happens? You make it happen. Each of you have the power to create this kind of discussion. Be the first one to share honestly, ask follow up questions when someone else shares, pray for your group members and reach out to them during the week, offer support when it's needed, let someone know that it's ok to not be ok, and for the love: let's all try and judge a little less. Honest discussion doesn't just happen. You make it happen.

1.   What has kept you from sharing honestly in the past? (Ex: shared once and people tried to fix me, fear, not wanting to reveal imperfections, etc.)

There are a few more questions for you to answer below to get an idea of your starting point as you begin this workbook. When you meet together with your group, you will have the opportunity to share your responses as part of your discussion time.

2.   Why did you decide to do this workbook?

3.   What are you hoping to get out of this workbook?

4.   What are you afraid of as you start this journey?

5.   Is there anything you want to get off your chest before the group starts?

6.   On a scale of 1-10, describe your relationship and connection to God. (By the way, there is no judgement here. Just be real.) 1-Distant, 10-Connected

                   1   2   3   4   5   6   7   8   9   10

7.   How can your other group members show you love throughout this journey?

15

Identity | A Soul Journey

VIDEO TEACHING

You'll end your weekly gatherings by watching the video teaching for the upcoming chapter.

THE PACE OF THE WORKBOOK

I am almost positive that each of you will go through this workbook and this journey at a different pace. A question that may be profound for one, may not be for another. It's important to mention this because although this workbook has a certain structure to it—daily content and weekly gatherings—I want each and every person to feel the freedom to go at their own pace.

While your group will continue meeting weekly to discuss the previous week's content, it is ok if you need to give more time and focus to a different section. For example, if you need to camp out on a question which prevents you from answering the rest of the questions in a chapter, that is ok. It will just mean that you won't be able to necessarily contribute to some of the discussion at that week's gathering. Or, if you answer each and every question and can contribute to each week's discussion—that is great, too. Ultimately, the hope is that you would allow God to lead you through this workbook at the specific pace that you specifically need. If you don't get to all of the questions that is absolutely fine.

If you find yourself "camped out" on a certain question or topic, I want to encourage you to share that with your group. I also want to encourage you to go back at some point and answer the questions you didn't get around to answering...even if that is weeks, months, or years from now.

Proverbs 24:27
"First plant your fields; then build your barn."

---

day two

THIS IS A SOUL-JOURNEY, NOT A BIBLE STUDY

Let me be very clear: I believe the Bible is 100% true and 100% God-breathed. I absolutely adore the Word of God. I believe the Bible is God's letter to us, a tangible gift to help guide, encourage and challenge us as we navigate life and faith. I need it and I think you need it too. With that being said, this workbook is more than just a Bible study.

While I think studying the Bible—knowing Bible verses and knowing what God has done over time—is incredibly important, I don't want the Word of God to just be knowledge to you (or to me). I want it to become real and personal to you and in order for something to become real and personal to you, it must intersect somehow with your life.

It's a lot easier to grow in our knowledge *about God* by studying the Bible. It's a lot harder to actually *know God* and allow Him to use the Bible to change and grow us. The latter requires vulnerability, letting go of control & comfort, time, humility, and trust. It's hard work, which is why I think often times we settle for just growing in our knowledge about God.

This workbook is meant to be a tool that helps the Bible, God, and your life collide. Throughout this workbook you will find a whole slew of personal questions intermixed with God's Truth. Don't be fooled: answering these personal questions and understanding yourself better is not a waste of time, and it is not less important than reading Scripture. Answering these personal questions is actually holy work, which was modeled to us by God himself.

In Genesis 3 we learn that Adam and Eve have done the one thing God told them not to do; they ate from the tree of the knowledge of good and evil. After they ate, filled with shame, they hid from God. In the verses that follow, God asks Adam and Eve a series of personal questions:

> *"But the Lord God called to the man, 'Where are you?' He answered, 'I heard you in the garden, and I was afraid because I was naked; so I hid.' And He said, 'Who told you that you were naked? Have you eaten from the tree that I commanded you not to eat from?' The man said, 'The woman you put here with me—she gave me some fruit from the tree, and I ate it.' Then the Lord God said to the woman, 'What is this you have done?' The woman said, 'The serpent deceived me, and I ate.'"*

Now, God knows everything. We can absolutely conclude that God is not asking these questions to grow in His own understanding. What God is doing here is extending an opportunity for Adam and Eve to face what they have done and grow in their own understanding of themselves. God places a high importance on knowing and understanding

17

ourselves and personal questions help us do that.

Personal questions help us confront the reality in our lives. For example: I may know in my head that God asks me to live humbly. That command becomes more real to me when questions surrounding humility in my own life get asked of me; In what ways do I live humbly? In what ways am I tempted toward pride?

Here, in this passage, God's questions not only cause Adam and Eve to confront their disobedience, but they also reveal some deeper realities in their hearts; they blame others for their actions, and they admit that they acted out of fear.

Personal questions have profound power to reveal, which allows us to see our great need for God in specific areas of our lives. This is exactly why this workbook has been written with so many personal questions for you to reflect on.

There is also another thing that happens when we answer these personal questions: our hearts become unburdened. I believe this was God's desire, too, when He asked personal questions of His own. When we respond honestly to questions, our hearts get lighter and the burdens slowly get lifted.

A FEW SUGGESTIONS

Below are some suggestions that I believe will help you get the most out of this workbook. The outcome will depend heavily on your attitude and posture going in. In other words, what you put into this workbook is what you'll get out of this workbook. God uses everything; it's up to us how much we allow Him to work:

Throw out any preconceived notions & expectations you have for a Bible Study.
This one is going to be most difficult for those of us who have been in churches and/or bible studies for a while. I want to encourage you to give this study a fair chance.We all have some sort of activity that at first we turned our noses up to, only to find out through experiencing it that we loved it. I'm not sure what pretenses you have about God, Christianity, or Bible Studies as you begin this workbook, and frankly, it doesn't really matter. What does matter is that you give yourself the opportunity to experience God and what He has for you throughout this study. This starts with letting go of your own agenda for this workbook and being open to what God might do — even if it's something new and unfamiliar.

Be honest with God, yourself & others (Don't show up in your "Sunday best")
God can't meet us personally if we aren't willing to be personal. So, I encourage you to show up with your whole selves. When you are journaling or reading the Bible or praying to God or sharing in your group, just be honest and real. I know there are hurts, pains, brokenness and junk in your life that you have tried so hard to hide. But the truth is, the

only way God can heal those parts of your life is if you bring those things out into the open for Him to heal. We can only be loved as much as we are willing to be seen. God is more pleased with an honest but messy answer, than an untrue, cleaned-up answer. (Group members and leaders, remember this when people are sharing! Celebrate honesty; don't reinforce performance-based sharing.)

Look for God in everything (Act as though God is speaking to you, rather than you just downloading information). God is alive, meaning God uses things in our everyday lives to speak to us. If we are reading the Bible or coming to our weekly gathering or trying a practice with an intent to hear from God, it will help heighten our awareness to Him and thus experience Him for ourselves. I'm not saying you will hear a booming voice from the heavens, but you might feel a tinge inside of you or see a word jump out to you or hear someone sharing something that is exactly what you are going through. These are all ways God speaks to us, and it's my hope that we learn to listen to all of the messages He has to share with us.

1. What is an example of something you know about but don't truly know? (i.e. some celebrity; you may know a lot about them, but not know them personally)

2. What are the feelings that come up when you read that this study is more than just a bible study?

    Why?

3. Is there a statement from this section that really sticks out to you? Why?

4. Which one of the suggestions is hardest for you to grasp? Why?

Identity | A Soul Journey

Galatians 5:25 (Suggested version: The Message)
"Since this is the kind of life we have chosen, the life of the Spirit,
let us make sure that we do not just hold it as an idea in our heads or a sentiment in
our hearts, but work out its implications in every detail of our lives."

DO THIS:

Reach out to one of your group members and see how their day is going.

day three

REMINDERS

I think it takes a lot of courage to look at our lives, recognize the things that are tearing us down, and not only want help, but actually seek help. This is exactly the journey you are about to embark upon, and I want you to know that I think you are brave and courageous for doing so. I also want you to give you a few reminders before you begin.

KNOW THIS: THIS GUIDE IS IMPERFECT.

Another woman, a living, breathing, human being wrote out these pages. What that means is it's imperfect. What that also means is it's real. Every exercise, bible verse, paragraph or question is something I did, read or experienced on my own journey. This book is a framework of the journey God has been leading me on toward transformation. My own personal journey has been written out and recorded in hopes that you might experience transformation too.

KNOW THIS: THIS GUIDE WILL JUST BE WORDS ON PAGES WITHOUT GOD.

I believe that true and lasting transformation happens only through the working of God's Spirit. You could do every practice perfectly, write out your honest thoughts and feelings, but without the power of the Holy Spirit, you will not change. Without the power of the Holy Spirit you will not change. To help you with this there will be a simple prayer at the start of every new section. This is there to help remind you of God's transforming power and invite that power to be with you on this journey. But, you are the only one that can choose to open yourself up to God, and that's what will need to happen if you want to experience change, freedom, healing and transformation.

KNOW THIS: GO EASY ON YOURSELF.

This isn't a guide to reveal all of your imperfections and feel terrible about yourself. As parts of yourself are revealed, especially the parts that you have tried so hard to hide, I want to remind you that God is a grace-filled God. You are loved and embraced smack dab in the middle of your junk. You don't need to get cleaned up before you come to Him. So, be nice to yourself. Ask God to give you grace and for His help to receive that grace. Face your struggles and imperfections with God; His gentle grace and unconditional love are enough to cover it all. Oh, and by the way, it is ok to cry. This workbook isn't the place for stuffing your emotions.

KNOW THIS: YOU ARE NOT ALONE.

Every single person on this planet has junk in their lives. We have all messed up; we have

Identity | A Soul Journey

all been hurt; we are all broken. If anyone tells you different, they are liars. Don't be afraid of being the only one. That is a lie that will just keep you cut off from experiencing God's transformation. You are not alone in this. I promise you.

KNOW THIS: THIS BOOK IS NOT MAGIC.

By the time you get through all these pages you will not be problem-free. Sorry. There's no magic bullet in this book that will rid you of all of your problems. But, I do believe, if you invite God to be with you and at work in you as you go on this journey, there are some wonderful things in store for you. Magic? No. Healing and transformation? Yes.

KNOW THIS: IT'S A JOURNEY.

You will read and hear about the term "journey" a lot in this book. Our life is a journey and so is this workbook. It is not something to conquer and summit, and the really good stuff is not at the end! The golden nuggets will be found in the midst of each step that you will take with God. There's no set destination to reach. It's like taking a leisurely flight —go up into the air, explore, see sights and enjoy the ride. What you leave with is what you saw along the way. So, take a deep breath and just be. Be where you are, and take each step as it comes. Explore the things that need to be explored. Don't race through this. Don't compete through it, either. God will reveal things to you in His time. He is in control. All you have to do is journey with Him.

KNOW THIS: GOD LOVES ALL OF YOU.

The last thing I want to tell you is that you are loved. God loves all of you. I have a dream that you and I will not only hear that message and trust it in our minds, but that we will believe it deep down into our soul. When we accept and embrace His unconditional love for us, we are able to live as the women God created us to be.

1.   Do any of the above statements seem difficult for you to believe or follow? Which ones, and why?

2.   Are there any statements that really resonate with you? Which ones and why?

John 3:17
"God sent his Son into the world not to judge the world,
but to save the world through him."

Chapter 1 | Preparing for the Journey

day four

CAPTURING YOUR STORY

A lot of this workbook is about uncovering, layer by layer, who you truly are. To begin that process of uncovering, you are going to write out a brief snapshot of your story.

If you've never written out your story, or shared your testimony before, here are some questions to help guide you:

Where was I born? What was my family life and upbringing like? Were there any major happenings that gave shape to who I am? When did I meet God? How has God changed me? What is my life like now? Have I experienced any major breakthroughs? Have I experienced any major tragedies or hardships? What is God teaching me? What is my relationship with God like now?

1. Begin to brainstorm and shape your story by jotting down answers to some of the above questions.

2. Open a Bible to Acts 26, verses 1 through 23. Here you will find record of Paul's story. Paul is the author of many of the New Testament books and we have a written account of his testimony to use as an example. The framework Paul used to tell his story is as follows:
   • My life before Jesus
   • When and how I met Jesus
   • My life since being in relationship with Jesus

23

Identity | A Soul Journey

3.   Using Paul's framework, write out your story below, incorporating some of the answers you jotted down from above. (If you haven't met Jesus yet, use the answers from the questions above to shape your story). Try and fit your story onto one page—sharing only the major nuggets of your life.

Acts 26:1-23

Chapter 1 | Preparing for the Journey

day five

PRACTICING YOUR STORY

At your weekly gathering, you are going to share your story with your group. Since the group time is limited, you will need to practice an abbreviated version of your story. Did you catch that? Practice!

Spend some time today and practice reading through your story out loud. As you practice, make sure your story stays around 5 minutes or less. In the coming weeks you will have several opportunities to share more details about your life. But, for now it is important to keep your story brief so that everyone has the opportunity to share.

Practice Tips:
- Read it out loud once.
- Make any necessary changes.
- Read it out loud again and time yourself.
- Cut out any parts that you need to.
- Read it out loud 1 to 2 more times.

Psalm 145:4-7
"Let each generation tell its children of your mighty acts; let them proclaim your power.
I will meditate on your majestic, glorious splendor and your wonderful miracles.
Your awe-inspiring deeds will be on every tongue; I will proclaim your greatness.
Everyone will share the story of your wonderful goodness;
they will sing with joy about your righteousness."

ACTION STEP:
Ask a man or woman, whose faith you admire, to share their story with you.

CHAPTER 2
Uncovering My Identity

notes

CHAPTER 2 VIDEO SESSION

Most of us have an issue with taking an honest look at our own lives

Two disclaimers:
- too much time spent looking at our lives can be a bad thing
- no time spent looking at our lives is perhaps even worse

Taking an honest look at our lives is a somewhat uncomfortable step of "pulling back the covers" and seeing what's there

Luke 15:11-32

Luke 15:17
"*But when he came to his senses...*"

We all have "pig slop" in our lives.

Change will not come without us coming to our senses and taking an honest look at our lives.

Jesus loves the lost.

PERSONAL NOTES:

Identity | A Soul Journey

introduction

UNCOVERING MY IDENTITY

When my sister and I were little girls, we would spend hours under an old olive tree in our front yard, overturning rocks and seeing what we could find underneath them.

Rollie pollies, spiders, ants, the occasional lizard and one time even a toad! We were in our own little adventure world; the Lewis and Clark of Ghallagher Court, pioneering the discovery of our front lawn. As we overturned rocks it became obvious which rocks hadn't been turned over in a long time because they were crawling with tiny little critters. The ground was usually cold and damp under those rocks, and it took time to discover all that was there (hence the hours referenced above).

Perhaps you spent your time doing something similar when you were younger. Exploring, discovering and uncovering your surroundings. This is what kids typically do. They are curious; they explore; and they're eager to learn. These activities and characteristics seem to fade as we grow into adulthood. The older we become, the less we seem to explore. We rarely take time to pause, look around and discover all the nooks and crannies of life. We just keep moving. We are convinced that there are more important things to be done than to sit around and uncover, and so our daily tasks and responsibilities take precedence.

This chapter has been written to give each one of you the opportunity to revert back to that childlike discovery. The hope is that you would push the pause button on life, so that you can uncover and explore who you are and who you know yourself to be.

Which "rocks" within you have been left untouched over the years? What might be hiding beneath them? Does it seem like a cold and desolate place to visit?

In this chapter you will find several pages of personal questions. Think of these questions like overturning rocks. Some questions will be reflective and allow space for you to elaborate. Other questions will offer simple checkboxes, a number scale, or a place for you to fill in the blank. The primary goal is that you answer these questions honestly.

A big part of healing, and thus the work of this chapter, is taking an honest look at our lives.

Lastly, don't get fooled into trying to write the perfect Christian answer. The only right answer is the honest answer. The more honest you are, the more you open yourself up to healing, transformation and freedom. There were some people back in the day that were always concerned with the perfect religious answer, and Jesus really disliked them. Let's not be like them.

Chapter 2 | Uncovering My Identity

Take a minute and ask God to be with you as you read through and fill out the following pages. This book and these words are not magic. Without God as our guide, they won't mean very much. We need God's love, power and grace in order to experience true transformation, healing, Truth, and freedom. Take a deep breath and turn your attention to Him as you begin this chapter.

PRAYER

God, I acknowledge that you are the one Who does the revealing, healing and transforming. And that is what I want. Will you use the words on these pages to speak to me, and will you be with me as I go through these pages? Lead me to what you want me to take a deeper look at, or something you want to show me.
Holy Spirit, help me to be open to God and His leading.
Give me the courage to be honest and open about myself. Amen.

Identity | A Soul Journey

day one

CHARACTERISTICS, ROLES, & DREAMS

For any questions you are unsure about, simply write, "I don't know," in the blank space. Also, remember: any honest answer is the right answer.

1. Who do I know myself to be now? What makes me, me? Pretend you are talking with me on the phone and we've never met before. How would you describe yourself? (i.e. what do you like to do? what makes you different from someone else? who/what has shaped you? what roles do you play?)

2. What qualities/characteristics/traits from the list below best describe you? Circle all the ones that fit you.

    Adventurous, affectionate, ambitious, angry, annoying, anxious, argumentative, arrogant, artsy, bossy, brave, brilliant, busy, calm, cautious, cheerful, compassionate, confident, considerate, courageous, crafty, critical, curious, decisive, dependable, determined, driven, diligent, dissatisfied, doubtful, eager, easygoing, efficient, encouraging, energetic, enthusiastic, faithful, fearless, frank, funny, gentle, giving, glamorous, greedy, happy, grouchy, helpful, honest, hospitable, humble, imaginative, impatient, impulsive, independent, intelligent, jealous, lazy, loving, loyal, mature, moody, naive, negative, nervous, obedient, observant, obsessive, opinionated, optimistic, peaceful, persevering, persistent, pessimistic, picky, polite, popular, positive, proud, quarrelsome, quick, quiet, rational, reliable, respectful, responsible, risk-taking, rowdy, rude, sarcastic, stingy, secretive, secure, self-centered, selfish, self-reliant, sensitive, silly, sincere, smart, sociable, stubborn, studious, talkative, thoughtful, timid, trusting, uncontrolled, warm, weak, wise, witty
    other:

Chapter 2 | Uncovering My Identity

3.   What roles do you play in your life?

○ Daughter   ○ Friend
○ Sister   ○ Teammate
○ Mother   ○ Caretaker
○ Aunt   ○ Student
○ Cousin   ○ Job: _____
○ Niece   ○ Volunteer Role(s)
○ Granddaughter   _____
○ Wife   ○ Other role:
○ Girlfriend   _____

4.   How are you/were you described in your family of origin? Do you/did you have a certain role that you play(ed) within your family?

○ the quiet one   ○ the strong one   ○ the rebellious one
○ the black sheep   ○ the positive one   ○ the achiever
○ the planner   ○ the negative one   ○ the funny one
○ the screw up   ○ happy-go-lucky   ○ other role:
○ the hero   ○ the star
                                               _____

a.   Do you (or did you) like this role?   YES   NO

b.   Does this (or did this) role affect your feelings of value as a person?

            YES   NO

If yes, how so?
      ○ I feel more valuable when I assume this role
      ○ I feel less valuable when I assume this role
      ○ I believe my value as a person, or in my family, is wrapped up in this role

c.   Do you know how that role developed? If so, describe how below.

d.   What sort of expectations are (or were) placed on you as a result of that/these role(s)?

Identity | A Soul Journey

e. Do you (or did you) like these expectations?

YES   NO   SORTA   Why, sorta?: _____

f. If you no longer live with your family of origin, have you continued to assume this role in your own family and/or adulthood?

YES   NO

Why or why not?

5. What are you good at?

a. What makes you good at this?

6. What are some things that you enjoy doing?

a. Is there anything that keeps you from doing the things that you enjoy?

7. What do you spend your time doing? Fill in the weekly calendar below with a sample of your schedule. (What's on your daily routine list?)
(ex: exercise, work, school, cleaning, eating, sleeping, extracurricular activities, friends, going out, time with God, church)

MONDAY	TUESDAY	WEDNESDAY	THURSDAY	FRIDAY	SATURDAY	SUNDAY

Chapter 2 | Uncovering My Identity

8.   What do you care about? What are your passions?

9.   How often do you engage with these passions or things you care about?

   ○ Consistently   ○ Once every year   ○ Rarely
   ○ Every once in a while ○ Once every year   ○ Never

   a.   What keeps you from engaging with these passions?

10.   Describe a time when you felt your heart beating fast and you were fully engaged. It was as if no matter what happened, you weren't going to move from that spot. (This could be in a conversation with someone, watching a movie, hearing a sermon, painting/creating, a trip, etc. Remember, any honest answer is the right answer!)

11.   What did you dream about becoming when you were younger?

   a.   Do you know why you wanted to become that? What was your reasoning behind that dream?

   b.   Do you still dream of becoming that?

            YES   NO

12.   What are your dreams now for yourself if you could do or be anything you want? (Pretend there are no stipulations.)

   ○ I'm living the dream!
   ○ I don't really know what my dream would be

      a.   Do you know why you don't know?

   ○ I think I'm too old to dream of becoming something.
   ○ I dream of becoming: _____

33

Identity | A Soul Journey

b. Are you in any way pursuing this dream? YES NO

c. If "NO", what keeps you from pursuing this dream?

13. What are you curious about that you haven't tried?

14. What is something you would do if you knew no one would judge you for it?

Proverbs 16:3
"Commit your work to the Lord, and your plans will be established."

ACTION STEP:

Plan a time to go do something you love; something that is core to who you are. Read a book, take a bath, go for a hike, play a sport, write poetry, paint, take pictures, etc.

34

Chapter 2 | Uncovering My Identity

day two

WORTH & VALUE

Our feelings of personal value have a drastic effect on our lives. Personal value is a feeling that causes us to believe we matter, or that we are worth something to someone. When someone shows care or concern for us, expresses love to us or for us, or acknowledges us in some way, we feel valuable, or valued. When we think we have something special to offer, or see something within us as special, this is value. As you answer the questions below, keep this idea of value in mind.

1. When you were in elementary, middle and high school, what made you feel valuable?

    a. Elementary/Childhood:
    I felt valuable when/I felt value from: _____

    _____

    b. Middle School/Early Teens:
    I felt valuable when/I felt value from: _____

    _____

    c. High School/Late Teens:
    I felt valuable when/I felt value from: _____

    _____

2. Do you still seek value from any of these areas today? If so, what and how?

3. What things have you been praised for in your life? Circle all that apply.

    Being good. Following rules. Being emotionally strong. Your looks. Your weight. Your grades. Your accomplishments. Your successes. Your job. Your kindness. Your intelligence. Being fun/funny. Being Driven. Being easygoing. Taking control. Being a leader. Independence. Having it all together. Other:

4. What do you think gives you worth and value? Phrased another way, what things, if taken away from you, would make you feel worthless or stripped of value?

    looks/appearance, job title, life accomplishments, life roles (mother, friend, daughter, wife, girlfriend), personality, success, body/weight, money, house/car

Identity | A Soul Journey

5.   On a scale of 1-10, how valuable do you feel on a day-to-day basis? (1 = of no value, 10 = completely valuable)

            1   2   3   4   5   6   7   8   9   10

6.   When do you feel most valuable?

7.   When do you feel least valuable?

8.   We all have an area of our life where we just want to be liked more. In what area of your life do you try to earn value? (ex: looks, job, role, spouse/marriage, accomplishments, romantic relationships, friendships/popularity, family)

9.   What sort of things do you do to earn your value in the above area(s)?
        (ex: exercise, shop, people please, never show emotions, achieve, work long hours, follow the rules)

10.   In what area(s) of your life do you feel not good enough?

        ◯ achievments   ◯ overall appearance   ◯ my body type
        ◯ family relationships   ◯ athletics   ◯ life choices
        ◯ my weight   ◯ my job/career   ◯ mistakes
        ◯ grades/school   ◯ romantic relationships   ◯ other: _____
        ◯ friendships   ◯ my purpose   _____

11.   How do you want others to see you?

        Pretty. Skinny. Successful. Athletic. Strong. Put-together. Driven. Smart.
        Creative. Artsy. Sensitive. Quiet. A Leader. Perfect. Kind. Other: _____

12.   What do you want to be known for?

Chapter 2 | Uncovering My Identity

13. What would be the worst thing someone could think or say about you?

14. What would be the best thing someone could think or say about you?

15. When do you feel the most beautiful? (While doing something specific? At a certain time of day? Through a certain action? When you achieve a certain look?)

   a. How do you describe that type of beauty? What is beauty to you?

16. Do you like who you are?

   HECK YES   NO WAY   SORTA

   a. Why or why not?

17. On a scale of 1 to 10, how well do you care for yourself? (1 = never even think about what I need, 10 = I seek balance, rest, work, and play)

   1   2   3   4   5   6   7   8   9   10

18. If you have an evening or some time to yourself, how do you spend it?

19. What are you most afraid of becoming?

20. What parts of yourself and/or your life do you hide from others?

   My marriage. How I really spend my time off. My obsession with social media. Overeating. Undereating. Control issues. Pride. Discontentment. Abuse. Strive for perfection. Yo-yo dieting. Anger. Shame for myself. Shame for others. Loneliness. Depression. Cutting. Thoughts of suicide. Feelings of insecurity. Lying. Judgment. Black and White Living. How much I compare myself to other women. Overspending. Never satisfied. Mistakes. My weight. Feelings of jealousy and/or envy. Addiction to drugs and/or alcohol. Other: _____.

37

Identity | A Soul Journey

21.   Do you have a secret that you have never told anyone about?

                        YES   NO

Just a reminder. You won't be forced to share this. However, we strongly believe that healing comes through relational sharing. This could be a great opportunity for you to share this part of your life in a safe setting. It seems too simple to be true, but healing does in fact start with sharing it out loud.

22.   What expectations are placed on you by others?

23.   What expectations do you place on yourself?

24.   Who knows you the best?

25.   Is there a common misconception that people have about you?

26.   Fill in the blank: "If people really knew me, they would know that _____

_____

Philippians 3:8
*"What is more, I consider everything a loss because of the surpassing worth of knowing Christ Jesus my Lord, for whose sake I have lost all things.
I consider them garbage, that I may gain Christ..."*

day three

CHILDHOOD

Here's the deal: we are born into a crazy world, vibrant and unique in our very own identity, and then things start to turn sour. People exclude us; we are made fun of; our dreams are crushed; people are mean; some of us face rejection, abandonment, abuse...basically, life happens, and along with it happening, our identities begin to warp, fade and conform. Our once vibrant and wide-eyed wonder is squelched within us, and we put on an armor to fight this dog-eat-dog world. We tell ourselves to be strong and keep going in hopes that soon enough we will be past our childhood and living vibrantly once again as adults.

Perhaps you have felt the same frustration I have felt when I became an adult and vibrancy did not come naturally. I soon realized that those parts of my childhood that I was so eager to move past and stuff down actually played a significant role in shaping me into the person I am today.

These moments, no matter how strong we were through them, had an effect on our lives, and we cannot deny that. Until we unpack and face our childhood hurts, wounds, suffering and pain, we will never be able to step into a Christ-like identity as adults.

1.   List out some positive aspects of your childhood. (ex: family dinners, vacations, communication, certain relationships, various memories)

2.   List out some negative aspects of your childhood. (ex: absent parents, abuse, alcoholic/addictive home life, scarcity, strict rules, divorce, abandonment, trauma, pressure)

Identity | A Soul Journey

3.   There may be some cross over from the previous two questions and this next question. That's okay. Below, your childhood is divided into three sections: birth to seven years old, eight years old to thirteen years old, and fourteen years old to eighteen years old.

         a.   For each section, write out 1-3 significant events/circumstances/ happenings that shaped you or changed you in some way.

            0-7

            8-13

            14-18

4.   On a scale of 1-10, how traumatic would you say your childhood was? (1 = fairly calm and peaceful, 10 = complete trauma and chaos)

     1   2   3   4   5   6   7   8   9   10

5.   Growing up, did you feel loved by your parents?

     YES   SORTA   NO

     a.   If yes/sorta, how?

     b.   If no/sorta, why not?

6.   Did you feel like you had to earn your parents' love by doing or achieving something? If yes, what was it?

Chapter 2 | Uncovering My Identity

7. How did that come about? Was this expectation to earn their love vocalized to you, felt through experience, or developed in some other way? (If you chose "some other way" please explain.)

8. Were there needs that you had that went unmet as a child? Circle all that apply.

encouragement, positive affirmation on my looks, acceptance of me for me, relieving the pressures of life, play time, freedom to pursue passions, safety, rules, togetherness, security, discussion/dialogue, Godly wisdom, talking about feeings, general guidance and direction, conflict resolution, comfort, protection, other:

9. What effect did those unmet needs have on you? Did you develop habits or responses to those unmet needs? For each thing you circled above, write it below and next to each unmet need write out a result or response you have or had from that unmet need. See example below.

Unmet Need ex: positive affirmation from father	Response ex: pursued affirmation from boys

10. How did these responses to your unmet needs effect the relationships in your life?

11. Think back on your childhood. Can you identify the age/grade/time when you first remember caring about what other people thought of you? Write about that instance below.

 a. Age/Grade:
 b. Who was involved?

 c. What did you want people to think of you?

41

Identity | A Soul Journey

d.   Do you know why you wanted people to think that about you?

e.   How did people respond?

f.   Do you remember how you felt?

g.   Do you still have this same desire for people to think something about you?

12.   What fears did you have growing up?

Psalm 68:5-6
"A father to the fatherless, a defender of widows, is God in his holy dwelling.
God sets the lonely in families, he leads out the prisoners with singing;"

---

day four

EVENTS, HAPPENINGS, & CIRCUMSTANCES

Throughout our lives, we experience certain events, happenings or circumstances that give shape to who we are. These events are often categorized as either positive or negative. For this next section, we are going to once again split up our adulthood by brackets of age. We are going to focus solely on the positive for this first portion.

POSITIVE EVENTS, HAPPENINGS AND CIRCUMSTANCES

1. Write down 1-3 positive events, happenings or circumstances for each age bracket below. You can skip any brackets that you haven't reached yet. (Ex: college, job, job promotion, marriage, relationship, award, accomplishment, baby, trip, opportunity.)

    19-26

    27-34

    35-42

    43-50

    51-58

    59-66

    67-74+

Identity | A Soul Journey

NEGATIVE EVENTS, HAPPENINGS AND CIRCUMSTANCES

2.   For this next section, we are going to focus solely on the negative events, happenings and circumstances in our lives.

We will address this later on, but I thought it necessary to just include a brief note about how much God cares about our pain and suffering. Whether it was self-inflicted or something that has happened to us, God's heart breaks over our heart breaking. Period. He does not stand at a distance and wait until we pull ourselves together. Instead, God cries with us, mourns with us and feels with us. (John 11:35) Although we want to know why things happen the way they do, that is not what will ultimately bring us hope and peace. God's presence with us in the pain is what brings us hope and peace. What I clung to after losing my sister was this: our world is broken, therefore I will experience the effects of brokenness, and that will feel terrible at times. But I claim the truth that God is bigger than any brokenness I experience. He will bring good (Romans 8:28, Genesis 50:20) from every terrible situation I encounter. God's presence with me in the pain is my hope. Will it negate the pain? No. Will it be a source of strength to face the pain? Yes.

Write down 1-3 negative events, happenings or circumstances for each age bracket below. You can skip any brackets that you haven't reached yet. (Ex: arrested, rehab, divorce, break-up, addiction, loss, a mistake, abuse, depression, abortion, miscarriage, loss of job/laid off, eating disorder, disease, marital conflict/crisis, financial crisis, sexual encounter, lying, stealing, accident, medical crisis, some sort of trouble you got into.)

19-26

27-34

35-42

43-50

51-58

59-66

67-74+

44

Chapter 2 | Uncovering My Identity

3. Have you shared this (or these) negative experience(s) with anyone?

                    YES   NO

a. If yes, who?

    • How did they respond?

    • How did you feel after sharing?

b. If no, why not?

    • How do you think you would feel if you shared these experiences with someone?

Romans 8:38-39
"For I am convinced that neither death nor life, neither angels nor demons,
neither the present nor the future, nor any powers, neither height nor depth,
nor anything else in all creation, will be able to separate us
from the love of God that is in Christ Jesus our Lord."

Identity | A Soul Journey

day five

FAITH & GOD

For some of us faith and God are integral parts of life. For others, an afterthought, a welcomed support system, or an on-the-shelf-as-needed type of thing. This section is a chance for you to uncover who God is to you and the role faith plays in your life.

1.   Briefly describe your relationship with God here. Do you know Him? When did you first meet Him? What has your relationship been like? What feelings do you have towards Him or about Him?

2.   Who is God to you?

3.   Who is Jesus to you?

4.   Who is the Holy Spirit to you?

5.   On a scale of 1 to 10 how close do you feel to God? (1 = completely distant, 10 = completely connected)

        1   2   3   4   5   6   7   8   9   10

6.   When do you feel furthest away from God?

7.   When do you feel closest to God?

46

Chapter 2 | Uncovering My Identity

8. What makes it difficult to connect with God? Circle those that apply.

    all of the pain in my life, my limited time, my view of Him, I don't think I need Him,
    I don't think He wants to spend time with me, I have a hard time viewing Him as
    a Father, other things are more important, distractions in life, the mistakes I've
    made, other: _____

9. Have you ever experienced God personally in your life? (i.e. felt His presence,
    felt Him speak to you, etc.) If so, describe a time here:

10. Circle how or where you experience God most. If you are unsure, circle the one
    that you think fits how you connect with God best:

    nature   people   worship   learning   serving   causes   alone time   don't know

11. What is one thing you would ask God, if He were sitting in front of you?

12. Are you angry at God for anything?   YES   NO

    a.   If yes, why?

    b.   Are you afraid of being angry at God? Why?

13. Have you processed your anger? If yes, how? If no, why not?

14. Have you experienced something traumatic or hurtful relating to God or church?
    Describe.

47

Identity | A Soul Journey

15.   Has this experience affected your concept of God? How?

16.   Is there anything you are trying to keep or hide from God?

Read Genesis 32:22-32
Jacob wrestles with God

DO THIS:
Text/call someone from your group and set up a time to get together (coffee, walk, etc).

CHAPTER 3
God-Given Identity

Identity | A Soul Journey

notes

CHAPTER 3 VIDEO SESSION

God-given identity: a specific and unique identity that God creates for each individual

Self-created identity: an identity that we, ourselves, create

4 ways that Ruth lives life out of the God-given identity:
    1. Ruth submits (Ruth 1:16 *"Don't urge me to leave you or to turn back from you. Where you go I will go, and where you stay I will stay. Your people will be my people and your God my God."*)
        • When we submit, God gives us a new perspective
    2. Ruth's position remains a position
    3. Ruth lives life as the woman she was wired to be (Ruth 2:10-12)
    4. Ruth lets God shape her through her circumstances

When we live life out of the God-given identity, we are led to purpose

PERSONAL NOTES:

introduction

GOD-GIVEN IDENTITY

Several years ago I met a woman who seemed to be miserable in her job, and in turn, miserable in life. She couldn't figure out what was wrong with her. Her connection to God was solid, she sought to live a life following God's leading, yet even still, something was missing. In an attempt to turn things around, she began practicing gratitude, took up a new hobby, enrolled in a gym nearby and poured herself into social functions. After some time, she felt an increase in happiness, but she still lacked a deep, inner sense of fulfillment.

One day she was asked to speak to a group of people about something she was passionate about. For the weeks leading up to this speaking engagement she studied and prepared and crafted a talk to communicate her passion in an effective way. Without even realizing it, as she prepared, something within her began to bloom.

Eventually it came time for her to deliver her message. It wasn't but a few seconds into her talk that she felt an overwhelming sense of fulfillment and joy bubbling up from within her soul—something she had been longing for for most of her life. Her joy and fulfillment seemed to grow more and more with each word she spoke, and if her emotions could have taken on a physical display, we would have had to peel her off the ceiling, she was so high on life.

What happened? What finally clicked?

You see, this woman had lived most of her life pursuing what others told her she was good at. By the time she was an adult, most of what she knew about herself were statements and conclusions that others had made about her. As an adult, she got a job in an area that other people told her would be a good fit, and she assumed life would begin to just fall into place. The problem was, her life was built mostly on others' perceptions of herself, rather than her own understanding of herself. She really didn't know who she was.

When she prepared that talk and delivered it, she uncovered parts of herself that she never knew—parts of herself that had been hardwired within her, knitted into her being, crafted into her soul as a piece of her God-given identity. And that fulfillment that she had been craving from various external sources seemed to come naturally from a place within her.

She was in her element, and it was good.

I know so much about this woman because that woman is me.

I lived for so many years doing things and pursuing things that others told me I would be good at. I chased after all the things our culture tells us are meaningful, yet the meaning and purpose never really came. When I began to uncover and live into my God-given identity, my life began radically changing for the better.

This is what our God-given identity can do.

The God-given identity has very little to do with the external life and almost everything to do with the inner life. It's a journey of learning that there is a you that is unique and separate from anyone else and that you is not something you created; it is someone God created. We are going to call this our God-given identity.

Let me be clear: the goal of these next two chapters is not to force an identity on you or simply tell you what to believe about identity. The goal of these next two chapters is to present the facts about two different types of identities so you can process it for yourself. You will decide for yourself which identity you want to live out of.

As you go through these chapters, underline statements that stand out to you, jot down questions that arise and take time to pause and reflect on how the statements apply to you. In other words, don't just read these chapters like a book, seeking to download information. I want you to make it personal. As you read, ask yourself these types of questions: "Is this true for me?" "How is this different from how I live my life?" "What does this statement mean for me?" "How would I apply that to my life?"

As always, I want us to take a minute to ask God to be with us as we go through this chapter. Will you pray with me?

PRAYER

God, I want to know what you have to say about identity. I want to hear,
with fresh ears, your truths and revelations about who you made me to be.
As I read these words, would you help write them on my heart?
Holy Spirit, help me draw the parallels to my life and see what you want me to see.
Speak to me; I'm listening. Amen.

Chapter 3 | God-Given identity

day one

THE FOUNDATION OF THE GOD-GIVEN IDENTITY

We each have a makeup of qualities, characteristics, passions, skills and experiences that give definition to who we are. This is what we know as our identity. In order to discover our personal identity, we must first learn about two different types of identity, how each is formed, and what they entail.

Those two types of identity are:

A self-created identity - an identity that we create

A God-given identity - an identity that God created and gives to us

For the next five days we are going to unpack and seek to understand the many facets of the **God-given identity**.

WHO IS THE GIVER OF THE GOD-GIVEN IDENTITY?

The main separation of the God-given identity from the self-created identity is that the God-given identity is given to us, not created by us.

This implies two things: 1) We have a giver. 2) That giver has something to give.

In the first few pages of the Bible, Moses writes about the creation of humans. Moses had encounters with God where God would impart knowledge to Moses for him to write down. This written account of the creation of humans is what we know as Genesis, the first book in the Bible. Let's read how the creation of humans is described by God and recorded by Moses:

Read Genesis 1:1-30.

Try reading this section in a few different versions of the Bible. If you don't have a Bible and/or different versions of the Bible, you can visit BibleGateway.com.

Choose two versions of the Bible from the list below and read Genesis 1:1-30 in each version:
- The New Living Translation
- The New International Version
- The Message
- The English Standard Version

53

Identity | A Soul Journey

1. Write out all the things that God made:

2. Fill in the blanks: "Then God said, let _____ make mankind _____ _____ _____, in our likeness..." Genesis 1:26 (NIV)

    A little side note: Circle the word, "us," in the above verse.

    This is our first encounter in the Bible with God, Jesus and the Holy Spirit. "Us" is the three together. Throughout the Bible we hear of the Trinity—the Godhead three in one. Basically, God, Jesus and the Holy Spirit are three distinct beings in one. Let's be honest, this whole three persons in one can be confusing. Anyone with me? I don't have the most eloquent answer to help you understand this, but I do have a metaphor that helps me wrap my mind around it. Consider water, ice and steam. All three of these are H2O, but in different forms and representing different characteristics of this compound. The same is true for God, Jesus and the Holy Spirit. All three are God in one, but each represent a different form of God.

3. So, who made mankind? Who made you? Who is "us" in the verse above?

WHAT OUR GIVERS HAVE TO GIVE
Now, let's read Genesis 1:27

> *"So God created man in His own image; in the image of God He created them; male and female He created them."*

4. Glance back through verses 1 - 26. Was anything else, besides mankind, created in the image or likeness of God, Jesus and the Holy Spirit?

We were created different from the animals, the earth, the light, the darkness. How? We were made to be like God. We were made in His likeness. One of the best descriptions I have heard in reference to being created in God's image is that we have been "filled up with the representation of God." (Benner, 2007)

Nothing else, except for humans, has been filled up with the representation of God. Nature, the sky, the animals, all of these may display God's beautiful workmanship, but God is not represented in the trees or the ocean or the animals.

God is, however, represented in us. We were formed to be like Him, to represent Him and to display who He is.

5. Have you ever had to represent someone or something? Describe that here so that you have a personal example of what representing means.

God has placed within each and every human being a representation of Himself (whether we acknowledge it or not).

You, my dear, have traits of God in you. You were made to resemble God.

Take a minute and just think about this. Close your eyes and think about your likeness to God. Imagine the God of the universe, who built the stars, dreamt up mountains and the sea, and consider the fact that God is represented within you. How does that make you feel?

6. Jot down any feelings that arose as you thought about being filled up with the representation of God:

THE CREATOR'S INTENT

My husband is an artist. A few years ago he created this painting called, "Bruised Water." I'm slightly obsessed with it. You might just be obsessed, too, when you hear about the painting's meaning. Take a look:

Before we learn about the meaning of the painting, let me ask you this: If it was your job to discover the true purpose behind this painting, to understand it and get a full description of it, who is the one person you would go to?

Did you say the artist?

Bingo. Only the creator of a painting can disclose that painting's true meaning and intent. Any other description would be a best guess, a paraphrase or a personal interpretation.

Identity | A Soul Journey

By the way, the artist's intent of this painting was to represent Christ's eyes as He looked upon us while on the Cross. Amazing, right?

The creator alone holds the meaning and intent of the created.

Let's think about this in light of our personal Creator.

God, our Creator, made us with a specific intention. Not only were we made to be filled up with the representation of God, we were also made uniquely to reflect God. When we look at ourselves or our lives, or when others look at us and our lives, it may not be obvious what our Creator's intent was in creating us. However, it does not take away from the fact that there is and was an intention when each of us were created. It only makes sense, then, that if we do in fact want to know what we were created for, how we were created and why we were created, that we seek the One who created us.

Only God, our personal creator, knows our true meaning, purpose and identity. We won't find our identity by seeking it ourselves or by trying to understand our characteristics and traits through an intense self-reflection.

The creator alone holds the meaning and intent of the created.

Genesis 1:27
"So God created mankind in his own image, in the image of God he created them; male and female he created them."

DO THIS:

Take some time right now, or later today, to call, text or email someone from your group. Check in and see how they are doing.

Chapter 3 | God-Given identity

day two
UNIQUE QUALITIES & CHARACTERISTICS

THE DIFFERENT PARTS OF OUR GOD-GIVEN IDENTITY

Our God-given identity is multifaceted. It isn't just wiring that was placed within us before we were born. Although that is part of our God-given identity. There are also elements of our identity that are formed and fashioned after we are born and continue forming throughout the course of our lives.

I've come up with an equation for our God-given identity. Take a glance, but know that we will spend the next few days unpacking each part of this equation in detail.

The equation for our God-given identity:

QUALITIES & CHARACTERISTICS + SPIRITUAL GIFTS + CHILDHOOD & EXPERIENCES + CONTINUAL TRANSFORMATION

= OUR GOD-GIVEN IDENTITY (WHICH LEADS TO PURPOSE IN OUR LIVES)

We are going to start with understanding the unique qualities and characteristics in the God-given identity for this section.

OUR UNIQUENESS

Think of someone, anyone.

1. Now list out a few things that make this person different from you:

It doesn't take much effort on our part to recognize that there is uniqueness all around us. I have a friend who is extremely similar to me. We think similar thoughts, like most of the same things and have a similar style. Still, we are not the same. There are a whole slew of things that set us apart from one another.

As mentioned before, I'm married to an artist. The more I get to know him through marriage the more I learn that creativity is hard-wired into his bones. He is creative at his core. It's part of who God made Him to be. What's interesting, though, is that in all the years he has been creating art, he has never created the same painting. Part of his creative expression requires that he create something new each time.

57

Identity | A Soul Journey

Our God is a creative God, the greatest artist of all time and the inventor of creativity. Doesn't it seem a bit ludicrous to think that the God who invented creativity would forgo creativity when creating His most prized possessions: humans?

As we learned earlier, humans weren't made like anything else God made. We were set apart, different, filled up with the representation of God. We are God's dearest creation.

Therefore, if God gave such unique and creative attention to the animals, the ocean, and the mountains, how much more care and creativity would He have given when creating us?

Look up Psalm 139:13-16 in your Bible.

> *"For You formed my inward parts;*
> *You covered me in my mother's womb.*
> *I will praise You, for I am fearfully and wonderfully made;*
> *Marvelous are Your works,*
> *And that my soul knows very well.*
> *My frame was not hidden from You,*
> *When I was made in secret,*
> *And skillfully wrought in the lowest parts of the earth.*
> *Your eyes saw my substance, being yet unformed.*
> *And in Your book they all were written,*
> *The days fashioned for me,*
> *When as yet there were none of them."*

I want us to camp out on two words for a minute. Those words are:

fearfully and *wonderfully*

Chances are if you have been connected to a church for sometime, you have heard this verse before. But, I want us to do more than hear this verse. I want us to understand what this verse is truly saying and let it trickle down into our souls.

Sometimes with different languages, words are used that have a widely understood meaning and context in one specific culture, but when translated into another language, the meaning gets a bit lost or cheapened. For this reason, it's important to look at the original language of our Bible verses from time to time to unpack exactly what the author was trying to get across.

Most of the Old Testament was originally written in Hebrew, while most of the New Testament was originally written in Greek. The Psalms were written mostly in Hebrew. Take a look at how the words "fearfully" and "wonderfully" are defined in the Hebrew language:

Chapter 3 | God-Given identity

Fearfully: Yare (yaw-ray) // things suited to produce reverence

2.   Look up the definition for "reverence" and write it out here:

Wonderfully: Palah (paw-law') // "apart" - set apart properly to distinguish or separate

3.   Look up the definition for "distinguish" and write it out here:

Here is a mashed-up translation of the verse Psalm 139:14:

I will praise you for I was made to produce reverence and to be set apart or distinguished.

4.   In your own words, write out your own mashed up translation of this verse:

I can't speak for you, but made "to be set apart," or made to be unique, packs a whole lot more punch for me than "fearfully" and "wonderfully." Being made wonderfully feels a little like a blanket statement, or a generality.

Being made to be set apart makes me feel special & prized. It makes me feel as if God took His time meticulously piecing me together, making sure that my wiring was completely unique and different from anyone else.

Every human being on this planet was made with special care and intention. There isn't one of us exactly like the other.

Short. Tall. Excited. Quiet. Thoughtful. Intuitive. Ambitious. Imaginative. Bold. Peaceful.

We are all unique.

Our uniqueness is displayed in our qualities, characteristics, passions, talents, and personalities, and it is these things that set us apart as different.

Later, in chapter seven, you will be guided through some practices to learn more about the unique qualities that God has placed within you and just how it is that He set you apart specifically. For now, just take in the fact that God has set you apart, uniquely.

WHAT'S SO GREAT ABOUT ME?

What's interesting are the words that come before "fearfully and wonderfully made."

Identity | A Soul Journey

5.   Look at Psalm 139:14 and fill in the blanks: "I will _____ _____
       _____ I am fearfully & wonderfully made."

Understanding how we were made should be so overwhelming that it causes us to praise God!

Let me be real for a moment: It is okay if your response when looking at and examining yourself is not praise to God. Not only do I not praise God all the time when I look at my-self, I take it a step further and sometimes question why God made me a certain way. For any of you who feel the same way, I want to remind you that you are not alone and these feelings are normal.

I also want to remind us, though, that if these are our feelings, then something is off. Something has gone awry. This is not the design for us when it comes to viewing ourselves. Instead of sinking into the temptation to curse or question God for how He made us, we must fight to understand why we withhold praise.

6.   What causes you to dislike, curse, or despise your unique creation? If you have an idea of what gets in the way, jot that down here:

Part of the work you will be doing in chapter five is processing the ways that we are held back from our God-given identity. So, it will help to have started your wheels turning on this.

Psalm 139:14
"I praise you because I am fearfully and wonderfully made;
your works are wonderful, I know that full well."

---

day three

SPIRITUAL GIFTS

Let's recap what we've covered thus far: We are all unique. We all have different qualities and characteristics placed within us by the very hands of God to set us apart.

OUR SPIRITUAL GIFTS

In addition to these qualities, we are also given spiritual gifts.

1.   Look up 1 Corinthians 12 in your Bible. What is the title of the section for verses 1-11?

2.   Who is the source of these "spiritual gifts?" (v. 4-11)

3.   List out the spiritual gifts described in this section, and also in Romans 12:4-8.

For every person who believes in Jesus Christ as their Savior and receives Him, they are given the gift of the Holy Spirit. In John 14:17, it says that the world (people who do not claim Jesus as their Savior), cannot accept the Holy Spirit because it neither sees Him nor knows Him.

When we receive Jesus as our Savior, we come to know the Holy Spirit over the course of our earthly lives.

> *"And I will ask the Father, and he will give you another Counselor to be with you forever - the Spirit of truth." John 14:16-17*

The Holy Spirit is described as a Counselor, a Helper, and an Advocate for us (John 14:16). It is through the Holy Spirit that each of us are also given spiritual gifts. (1 Corinthians 12:4-11)

4.   Can you describe, in your own words, why these spiritual gifts are given to us? (Hint: look at 1 Corinthians 12:7 - the NLT version is my favorite translation)

Identity | A Soul Journey

Another word on the spiritual gifts given to us is found in the notes of 1 Corinthians 1:7. It says this:

"A spiritual gift is some capability given through the Holy Spirit that enables one to minister to the needs of Christ's body, the church. The greek word used here stresses that it is a gift of grace. This means, we don't do anything to earn it or deserve it, but rather it is given to us as a pure gift." (NIV Study Bible)

A gift of grace.

Every single believer is given gifts from the Spirit to equip them to be involved in God's work. These gifts are not earned or merited. They are given as gifts of grace, and their purpose is not to puff ourselves up and become great. Their purpose is to help us serve God's people, and point back to the greatness of God.

I just want to take a minute and remind you, dear, that the moment you receive (or received) Jesus, you are given spiritual gifts. There are no exceptions. Your age does not matter, your past does not matter, your intellect and level of education do not matter. The Bible is very clear that every believer is given spiritual gifts. God doesn't withhold gifts from any of His sons and daughters. So, just in case you had any thoughts in your mind about being omitted from God's gift giving, I would like to kindly tell you that you are wrong. You, sister in Christ, have been given spiritual gifts and God has great plans to use you and your spiritual gifts to reach the needs of His people.

If you aren't a follower of Jesus, you are off the hook for the question below! If you want instead, turn to pages 156 & 157 to learn more about what it means to be a follower of Jesus.

5.   For those of you who are followers of Jesus, take an online spiritual gifts test to determine your spiritual gifts! There are several free options online. Simply type into a search engine: "free spiritual gifts test" and record your results below.

---

1 Corinthians 12:7
"Now to each one the manifestation of the Spirit is given for the common good."

Chapter 3 | God-Given identity

day four

CHILDHOOD & EXPERIENCES

What about the things that happen to us, the experiences we go through, the choices—both positive and negative—that we make? How do these fit into our God-given identity?

There are certain things that happen to us in our life, and these things shape us in profound ways. They change us at our core and our identity transforms. It's important to acknowledge the presence of these happenings and identify the ways they've shaped us. It's also important to note that these experiences don't detract from our value or add to our value, but they have the power to make us feel that way if we leave them unexplored.

I will not pretend to know God's role in the hardships, trials and pain that we endure while here on this earth. I don't think there is a simplified answer. What I do know is that God is completely good, so in Him there is no evil and He can cause no evil. I also know that when we experience pain, evil and hardship, God promises not to waste our pain. He promises to bring good from every terrible situation if we let him.

> *"You intended to harm me, but God intended it for good to accomplish what is now being done, the saving of many lives."* Genesis 50:20

I find it important to include that the words spoken above came from a guy who was sold into slavery by his own brothers and was thrown into jail due to a false claim. This man had every right to shout from the rooftops "this isn't fair!" But, he didn't. He knew that His God was in control and had a plan to use everything for good.

Just in case you were still unsure about the unfair, terrible, painful happenings in life, here are some other words, spoken by another guy who was stoned, beaten, attacked by a mob, and shipwrecked (just to name a few of his sufferings):

> *"And we know that in all things God works for the good of those who love him, who have been called according to his purpose."* Romans 8:28

This is the same guy who wrote letters to his people encouraging them to rejoice...while he was in jail. I think you can agree that this type of perspective can only be achieved through God.

As with so many of the other components of our identity, we need God to help guide us and lead us through our experiences so that He can use them for good and bring some sense of purpose from them.

Sometimes we can be tempted to move quickly past the hardships in our lives. It's easy

63

Identity | A Soul Journey

and perhaps even encouraged in our society to stuff them down, pretend they didn't happen and try to forget about them.

God wants the opposite. God wants us to fully process these moments with Him. He wants to walk us through what happened, allow time and space for us to feel and grieve the pain and loss and then let Him form something good from it.

1. Which experiences in your life have you quickly moved past, stuffed down or tried to forget?

I have a dear friend who suffered through an eating disorder in college. She has since healed from the depths of her struggle and has said to me that she has watched God bring good from this dark pit of struggle. God's healing of this season of her life has propelled her toward a career of counseling people through their own struggle with eating disorders. She gets to provide hope and healing in a way that most people couldn't because she understands it, she walked with God through it, and God has brought her freedom from it.

I have another dear sister in Christ who lost her daughter to drug addiction. She now sits on the board of a recovery home for women who are rebuilding their lives from the dark depths of drug addiction and prostitution. She gets to play a role in women being set free. This is all because she was courageous enough to walk through the pain with God, not run from it or stuff it down, and God is bringing good things from it.

Honestly, I could fill this entire book with stories like this because this is what our God does. He takes our experiences, offers us a journey of healing and brings forth purpose. about being omitted from God's gift giving, I would like to kindly tell you that you are wrong. You, sister in Christ, have been given spiritual gifts and God has great plans to use you and your spiritual gifts to reach the needs of His people.

Our God-given identity is a holistic identity. It encompasses us as a whole person--- experiences, gifts, characteristics, events, wiring, both the positive and the negative. God uses everything in our lives for a great purpose. Nothing is wasted. But, we play a role in that. We must be willing to let God take us back to the pain, give him permission to lead us through it, and allow him to heal us properly.

2. Is there an area of your life that comes to mind as a place that needs some proper healing?

Genesis 50:20
"You intended to harm me, but God intended it for good to accomplish what is now being done, the saving of many lives."

---

day five

TRANSFORMATION & PURPOSE

OUR TRANSFORMATION

Clearly you aren't the same person you were 10 years ago, or five years ago, or even one year ago. Change and transformation are very natural parts of life. Even the very cells of our body replace themselves every seven years! Your unique characteristics and spiritual gifts will morph and mature or take on new shape as your life progresses. Even how you interpret and what you learn from a negative or positive experience will change over time.

What does this mean for our larger God-given identity as a whole? Does our God-given identity change?

Transformation is at the core of the GLAM ministry because we believe it is at the core of God's heart and God's design for our earthly lives. It would be a crying shame to make a decision to accept Jesus only to remain stagnant in your faith and spiritual development for the rest of your life.

God not only dreamt up and created the process of transformation, He has designed the fullness of our life with Him to come by way of transformation.

Did you catch that? The fullness of our life comes by way of transformation.

> *"...I have come that they may have life, and have it to the full."* John 10:10

Let's read what is written about transformation in the Bible:

> *And we all, with unveiled faces, beholding the glory of the Lord, are being transformed into the same image from one degree of glory to another. For this comes from the Lord who is the Spirit.* 2 Corinthians 3:18

> *Therefore, I urge you, brothers and sisters, in view of God's mercy, to offer your bodies as a living sacrifice, holy and pleasing to God—this is your true and proper worship. Do not conform to the pattern of this world, but be transformed by the renewing of your mind. Then you will be able to test and approve what God's will is—his good, pleasing and perfect will.* Romans 12:1-2

God's transformation is not about salvation. We can accept Jesus as our Savior, and refuse His transformation throughout the course of our lives. What we will miss out on is not eternity, but rather the fullness of our lives here on this earth.

Remember at the beginning of this workbook, I talked about our identity being a steering

Identity | A Soul Journey

mechanism for our life. It has the power to steer us down paths of abundance or paths of deprivation. This is where that comes into play. The God-Given identity transforms over time from one degree of God's glory to another. This transformation leads us to abundance and fullness here on this earth.

In the two verses listed above, the same Greek word is used for be/being transformed. That Greek word is: metamorphóō. Say it out loud...it's kinda fun...met-am-or-fo'-o.

Now, take a look at how the word is broken down:

> metá - change afterward, change after being with
> morphóō - form embodying inner essence

Put it together and this is what we get:
> metamorphóō: inner change after being with (God)

Metamorphóō is God's design and plan for our transformation---that we would undergo inner change after being with Him. Glance back up to those verses listed above and re-read them with this definition for "transformed" in mind.

Can you guess which English word comes from this Greek word? Think back to elementary school...

Metamorphosis!

Don't you remember that sweet little book "The Very Hungry Caterpillar," or, perhaps you remember an elementary school science class in which you watched, before your very own eyes, as a caterpillar morphed into a butterfly.

Just to refresh our minds, here is the metamorphosis process explained:
> Stage 1: A butterfly lays an egg.
> Stage 2: The egg hatches into a caterpillar.
> Stage 3: The caterpillar grows.
> Stage 4: The caterpillar makes a cocoon.
> Stage 5: The caterpillar is dormant and in a resting stage while *transforming* into a butterfly.
> Stage 6: The caterpillar is completely transformed into a butterfly and emerges from the cocoon.

This metamorphosis is an incredible visual we have been given for our own life-long process of transformation.

I liken our decision to receive Jesus as our Savior to the process of entering the cocoon. From the outside, it might look pretty boring—not a lot going on except some cocooning. But, on the inside, major action is happening. Inside the cocoon, the caterpillar is undergoing a remarkable transformation. I consider this cocoon stage to be the course of our lives. Once the caterpillar has done all of its changing and transforming inside the cocoon, it comes time for the butterfly to emerge. This would be the time we leave this earth and enter into Heaven.

BEING TRANSFORMED/TRANSFORMING

*"Do not conform to the pattern of this world, but **be transformed** by the renewing of your mind."* Romans 12:2

> In the notes section of my Bible for Romans 12:1-2, it says this in regards to being transformed: "a lifelong journey of returning to our glorified state." (NIV Study Bible)

Remember at the beginning of our workbook when we talked about our lives and this workbook being a journey, not a mountain-top summit? Here, in this verse, is where you will find some of the heart behind that.

Our life is one giant process of metamorphosis. We are continually being transformed. God is transforming us from one degree of glory to another. It's not about summits or mastery or achievements while we are on earth. It's an imperfect process, an unfolding, a transforming into the God-given identity He has created within us. And it takes time—our entire time here on this earth, to realize it's completion.

The fullness of our lives, God's continual transformation, is the lifelong journey of returning to our God-given identity, our glorified state.

1.   Can you think of an area of your life that you have felt a sense of transformation taking place? (For example: I lived most of my life trying to control everything and essentially believing that I could live life without mistakes. That is until one day when I made a mistake that I didn't mean to and it was serious. I had to confront my own imperfections and need for grace head on. Since then, God has been transforming my legalistic and controlling nature into a spirit of grace and forgiveness.)

OUR TRANSFORMER

This is important for us to remember while we look at the areas of struggle and brokenness in our lives. If you are anything like me, you want to develop a quick, stepby-step plan to eliminate the brokenness in your life. God's plan of transformation is quite different. It's a deep, healing process that takes time. And we are not the ones in control of our transformation; He is.

Perhaps you are already one step ahead of me, but doesn't this whole transformation process beg the question, "Just who is it that does the transforming within us?"

67

Does transformation take place as a result of will-power? Are the most holy people the ones that transform?

> Michelangelo, a famous artist from the 1500s, once said while talking about his process of sculpting, "Every block of stone has a statue inside it and it is the task of the sculptor to discover it."
>
> He was implying that there was a statue already formed within the block of stone just waiting to be uncovered. He described his role as the sculptor as taking away, not adding on.

An important part to note about this God-given identity is that it is not intrinsic knowledge. From the moment we are born we don't automatically know our characteristics, what makes us unique, what our spiritual gifts are and what passions we possess. God's design was, and is, for us to come to Him over our lifetime to learn and receive who He made us to be and to let Him be the one to grow and transform us into our identity. He has our identity within Him ready to give to us when we come to Him to receive it.

This is where that phrase "find your identity in Christ" comes from.

We find our identity by being in relationship with God and going to Him to receive wisdom and understanding about who we were made to be.

Uncovering who God made us to be will be a transformation that takes place over the course of our life as we seek God more and more.

Your identity, the woman God created you to be, has already been created. It's wired into the fibers of your being. You don't need add-ons to find your identity or to live a fulfilled life. You need God, your Sculptor, to help you chip away at the stone around you so the woman you were made to be can be revealed. That chipping away, your metamorphóō, will happen over the course of your life as you learn to yield yourself to God's transforming power.

THE GOD-GIVEN IDENTITY LEADS US TO OUR EARTHLY PURPOSE

Let's recap:
- God created us uniquely.
- God has given us spiritual gifts.
- Our childhoods and experiences give shape to our God-given Identity.
- God's design for life is transformation, and He does the transforming.

Now, we are going to explore our specific purpose as it relates to our God-given identity.

> *"For we are God's handiwork, created in Christ Jesus to do good works, which God prepared in advance for us to do."* Ephesians 2:10

Remember in the introduction to this workbook, I talked about our identity being a sort of steering mechanism for our lives? This is completely true of our God-given identity.

In addition to the God-Given Identity steering your life toward abundance and fullness, knowing and understanding your God-given identity will also steer your life toward your God-given purpose.

The God-given identity uses our uniqueness, our spiritual gifts and the situations we have experienced to reveal our purpose in life and how we pursue that purpose.

Take a look at this diagram:

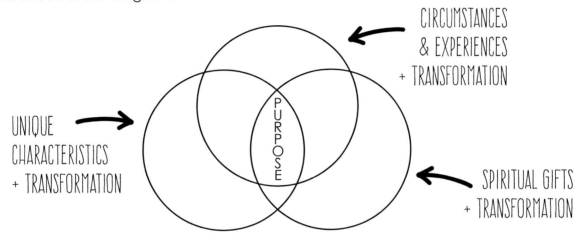

Through the process of understanding and embracing our entire God-given identity, we are led toward our purposes here on earth.

Often times we are lured toward seeking our purpose before understanding our identity. God's design is for us to receive the identity He has for us so that we can be led to our God-given purpose in life.

If a computer is wired to compute, its purpose will be revealed once we understand how it was wired. The same is true for most everything. When we understand how something was made, we can better understand the purpose for which it should be used.

THE GOD-GIVEN IDENTITY IS THE BIRTHPLACE FOR PURPOSE

Uncover how God wired you, and you will soon uncover the purpose for which you were wired.

To come full circle on our God-given identity, I want to remind us that when we are living life out of our God-given identity, fulfillment and satisfaction will come naturally. We won't have to frantically search after fulfillment. We can experience fulfillment and satisfaction as our identity is revealed and unfolded with God and we step more and more into who we truly are.

Identity | A Soul Journey

And remember, God gives us a WHOLE identity. He has a plan and purpose for everything. Nothing about you is a mistake in God. Nothing will be wasted with God.

This is our God-given identity.

Colossians 1:16-17 (MSG)
"For everything, absolutely everything, above and below, visible and invisible, rank after rank after rank of angels—everything got started in him and finds its purpose in him. He was there before any of it came into existence and holds it all together right up to this moment."

ACTION STEP:

Pick up some seeds and plant them. Or, buy a small plant from the store. Water it, give it sunlight and watch it grow and transform over time. You could even write the word "transformation" on the pot to remind you of a tangible example of what it looks like to transform.

CHAPTER 4
Self-Created Identity

Identity | A Soul Journey

notes
CHAPTER 4 VIDEO SESSION

Self-created identity: an identity that we, ourselves, create

Parallel the same four categories we looked at last week in the life of Ruth:
1. Submission to God
2. Position & Roles
3. Inner-wiring
4. Life circumstances

Genesis 3:1-6 The life of Eve
1. Eve takes
   • Not Enough: She believed the lie that what she had was not enough
2. Eve's position was not enough (Genesis 3:6)
3. Eve malfunctions ("She also gave some to her husband, who was with her, and he ate it.")
4. Eve leans away from God in negative circumstances

God is in the business of redemption

PERSONAL NOTES:

introduction

SELF-CREATED IDENTITY

I worked as a pastor to middle school students for several years. Every Thursday, we would open our church doors for any middle school students who wanted to come, hang out and play games. What drew the students in each week was free pizza. We would order stacks of pizza as a way to love students in their native language: food.

This one particular Thursday afternoon I saw one of our students from far up the street sprinting toward the church. This kid was in a hurry. He frantically entered the building, eyes darting all over the place, desperately in search of something. It wasn't long before I realized that something was pizza. Once he spotted the stack of pizza boxes, he ran up to the table, grabbed a box, flipped open the top and snatched a piece of pizza like it was a million dollars. I swear it was as if his eyes were tenderly hugging the pizza. What then followed was the fastest consumption of pizza I have ever witnessed. But, something interesting happened about halfway through his consumption of that slice of pizza. With one hand he was shoving a slice of pizza into his mouth, and with the other hand he was picking up a second slice of pizza and raising it high enough so that he could stare at it while inhaling the first slice! I LOVE middle schoolers. They do what we all wish we could do and they don't care!

What's funny is that some adults read that story and laugh demeaningly. But, replace the word "pizza" with "iPhone," and the playing fields have just been leveled.

The truth is, we all have a "pizza."

We all have something (or some things) that we frantically chase after in search of fulfillment.

> It may be a tangible item I have: a certain body type, money, a car, clothes, a house, a husband/boyfriend

> Or, it may be something I do: a job, an accomplishment I achieve, roles I play, weight I gain or lose

> Or, it may be what others say about me: she's pretty/sexy/beautiful, likable, a "good girl," successful, athletic, smart

How often do we sprint toward one of these things listed above, sure that it will mean we have arrived in life? We aren't even midway through inhaling that something and we have our sights set on the next thing to bring us fulfillment, and we begin the cycle all over again.

Identity | A Soul Journey

Sometimes I will be eating breakfast, thinking about what I will have for lunch. Other times I'll be dreaming up what vacation to take...while on vacation.

We live in such a way that seeks satisfaction from "out there" somewhere. We believe fulfillment in life will come from the accumulation or consumption of things, statuses or appearances.

Not only do we seek fulfillment from these categories, but we also place the sum of our being in these categories: I am what I have, what I do, and/or what others say about me.

When we get asked about who we are, we tend to list off all of the things that we think make us important. What we have, what we do, and what others say about us is the source of our value and who we know ourselves to be. This is what we are going to call our self-created identities.

This next chapter unpacks and reveals the various parts of the self-created identity. I am 99.9% sure that every human being lives some part of their life out of a self-created Identity (yes—even the most committed Christian, too). We all have places of our lives that we have placed the sum of our being in, or qualities we have adopted in an attempt to win ourselves value.

As you work through the sections for this chapter, be aware of how it relates to you. Underline statements that stand out to you, jot down questions that arise and take time to pause and reflect on how the statements apply to you.

Let's take a minute to ask God to be with us as we go through this chapter.

PRAYER

God, I need your help to not get defensive as truths about the self-created identity are revealed. Can you cover me with grace and acceptance as I read these words and compare them to my life? Show me the truths I need to hear, and the aspects of the self-created identity that I have adopted into my own life.
I'm ready to hear from you. Amen.

---

day one

THE FOUNDATION OF THE SELF-CREATED IDENTITY

Just as it was with our God-given identity, there are a few things we can imply when looking at our self-created identity.

The main difference of the self-created identity is that we are the source and creator of it. Our identity is not something given to us, but rather created by us.

With the God-given identity, God is our creator, and He has created us with specific and unique qualities, characteristics and gifts. He is the one to reveal and uncover that uniqueness created within us through the process of transformation throughout our entire lives.

The self-created identity forms and fashions various qualities, characteristics and gifts as the self desires.

HOW IT'S FORMED

When we come into this world, we are each born into a specific culture, family or family system.

It's important to highlight and talk about culture & family because they are the biggest influencers of our self-created identity.

As we grow up, we begin to form our identity—who we are and how we fit into the world. This comes by way of observation, trial and error and encounters with the people and culture around us. Each culture and family has a particular set of beliefs, systems and measures regarding someone's personal value. Naturally, as we all desire to live a life of value, we observe the things our culture and the people around us find value in, and we begin to create our personal identities out of these things.

Thomas Keating describes this as "a best guess at what we need in order to feel good about ourselves." Our self-created identity is formed as a response to the need within us to have personal value.

It's important to note that the American culture seeks value primarily in external and outer appearances. In other words, what is judged and measured are the things that people can see, not the inner parts of someone's being. A good amount of families also place a high value on the external, and give little attention to the internal qualities of a person. Because of this, our self-created identity ends up being primarily focused on the external.

75

Identity | A Soul Journey

Henri Nouwen categorized the world's system of value by these three categories:

- What a person does
- What a person has
- What others say about a person

These become the categories out of which our self-created identities are formed.

Romans 8:6-8
"Obsession with self in these matters is a dead end; attention to God leads us out
into the open, into a spacious, free life. Focusing on the self is the opposite
of focusing on God. Anyone completely absorbed in self ignores God,
ends up thinking more about self than God. That person ignores who God is and
what he is doing. And God isn't pleased at being ignored."

ACTION STEP:

While watching TV, or anytime you see an advertisement: 1. determine what product they are selling (hair product? beer? food?), 2. determine what they are using to sell it (a woman's body? smiles? relationship? a celebrity?), 3. determine the underlying message being portrayed through the advertisement (buy our product and you'll get a boyfriend? buy our product and you'll be prettier?).

day two
QUALITIES & CHARACTERISTICS

THE DIFFERENT PARTS OF OUR SELF-CREATED IDENTITY

I've created an equation for the various parts of the self-created identity:

QUALITIES & CHARACTERISTICS + PASSION, SKILLS & INTERESTS + CHILDHOOD & EXPERIENCES + PERFORMANCE & PERFECTION

= THE SELF-CREATED IDENTITY

QUALITIES & CHARACTERISTICS

As opposed to the God-given identity, which takes a deeper look within ourselves and discovers what unique qualities and characteristics lie there, the self-created identity looks around and adopts the celebrated qualities and characteristics that are widely valued in the culture around us, whether or not they come naturally to us.

1.   Take a second and think about the culture in which you live. Can you list out a few qualities and characteristics your culture sees as valuable? Here are just a few that come to mind for me and the American culture:
(ex: powerful, thin, attractive)

2.   What do you think your parents/guardian saw as valuable in you? Or, what sort of qualities did it seem your parents/guardians valued in a person?
(ex: rule-follower, extrovert, emotionally strong, kind, happy, smart)

3.   Can you remember the first time you personally noticed a quality or characteristic that was valued in our culture or valued by people around you? What was it?

Identity | A Soul Journey

4.   Did this change the way you lived your life or viewed yourself in any way?

5.   Describe the first time you remember doing something to get the approval or praise from someone. What did you do?

      a.   Who were you seeking praise from?

        • Did it work?

        • How did you feel?

        • Did it feel in line with who you are?

If you display the qualities and characteristics our culture sees as valuable, you are likely to feel a positive sense of personal value and thus maintain your self-created identity.

But, what happens if you don't display those qualities approved by culture and people? Most often, you are likely to feel a lack of personal value, prompting you to hide the parts of yourself that are seen as less valuable, or fix and/or improve parts of yourself.

6.   List out some qualities and characteristics our culture sees as less valuable. (ex: weak, overweight, unpopular, etc.)

7.   Can you also list out a few things your parents/guardians and the people around you saw as less valuable?

8.   Can you remember a time when you felt the lack of approval or acceptance from people or culture? What happened?

Chapter 4 | Self-Created Identity

• How did you feel?

• Did you hide this part of you? Or, did you seek to change this part of you?

Later we will read how some of these self-created characteristics may, in fact, be part of who God made you to be. They aren't all false. For example, God may have made you to be a driven person and being driven is something our culture sees as valuable. It isn't bad to use that drive in life. But, the crucial part is recognizing that being driven is part of you, not the sum of your entire being or the place from which you derive value. Therefore it doesn't define you, it doesn't give you worth, and it doesn't take away your worth. It's simply a part to your greater whole.

When it comes to our self-created identities, our culture, the people around us and we, ourselves, can sometimes place the sum of our being in these things and either add or detract our personal value based on them.

In a sense, there are qualities that we believe make us valuable, and if we were to lose them, our personal value would decrease.

9. What quality, characteristics, experience, or role in your life have you attached your personal value to? Or, phrased another way, what quality, characteristics, experience, or role in your life that if lost would make you feel less valuable?

What God intends for our qualities and characteristics that are innate within us, is that we would receive and experience joy when we express those qualities, but refrain from placing our value as a person in those qualities.

Romans 12:2
"Do not conform to the pattern of this world, but be transformed by the renewing of your mind. Then you will be able to test and approve what God's will is—his good, pleasing and perfect will."

Identity | A Soul Journey

day three

PASSIONS, SKILLS & INTERESTS

PASSIONS, SKILLS & INTERESTS

In addition to our culture and the people around us valuing certain qualities and characteristics, there are also passions, interests and skills that are seen as more or less valuable.

I remember talking to a young woman who was a senior in high school about her passion for theater. She had been in several musicals over the years and I wanted to know more about it. Her face lit up when I asked her questions, and with each answer her eyes widened as she told me the different roles she had played, the songs she sang and the costumes she wore. Knowing that she was approaching graduation, I asked if she was planning on studying theater in college. It was like someone turned off the lights to her show. Her eyes grew dim, her shoulders sank, and her hands fell to her side. Quickly, she replied, "No. It's not a realistic major. I won't be able to make money off of that."

Theater was seeping out of this dear gal's soul, yet somewhere along the way she was told, or she observed in the adults around her, that passions are fine to pursue as long as they make you money and offer a realistic career path.

In other words, having a passion for something is great, but only certain types of passions are acceptable to pursue.

1.   List some passions, skills and interests you think your culture values:

2.   How about passions, skills and interests you think your family of origin values:

3.   Is there a passion, interest or skill that you have hidden or neglected because it didn't seem realistic, valuable or worthy to pursue?

4.   Think about some of the things you do in your daily life (work, school, relationships, hobbies, recreation, etc.). If you could really choose, would you still pursue these things?

80

Chapter 4 | Self-Created Identity

- Do they bring you joy, reward you in any way, or provide for a basic need?

- Are there any that you are doing for others, or simply because it is more accepted in the culture?

5. Is there an innate passion, skill or interest in your life that you have pursued? Why did you pursue it? How did it feel?

6. If you could really choose, is there a passion, skill or interest that you would want to pursue?

Psalm 37:4
"Delight yourself in the Lord and He will give you the desires of your heart."

DO THIS:
Pray for one, a few, or all of the women in your group.

day four
CHILDHOOD & EXPERIENCES

NEGATIVE & POSITIVE EXPERIENCES + CHILDHOOD

Up to this point in our self-created identity, we have had the power to choose. We can choose to adopt certain qualities, hide various passions, learn new skills and be in control of forming an identity that we believe will win us value.

But, what about the things that happen to us?

Sexual abuse. Depression. Loss. Bullying. Miscarriage. Broken home life. Divorce.

What happens to our self-created identity in these circumstances? Both the negative and positive circumstances we go through in life have the power to add or detract to our personal value when it comes to the self-created identity.

I know so many women who have been sexually abused and yet rarely talk about it. I know there are a number of reasons for this, but I can't help but think our culture is partly at fault. While I think we are getting better at talking about sexual abuse as a society, I still think we have a long way to go in the realm of talking about real life trials, tragedies, and pain.

When we ignore or hush certain experiences that a person goes through, we send the message that it's too messy to handle...or worse, that the person who experienced such difficulty is too messy to handle.

As a result, when a person is living out of their self-created identity they tend to cover up the negative circumstances, events and happenings to prevent shame and decreased personal value.

On the flip side, our self-created identities encourage us to project the positive circumstances, events and happenings as the means by which we receive a sense of pride and increased value.

Our attempt to maintain our personal value through hiding and projecting is like a lifelong teeter-totter of shame and pride.

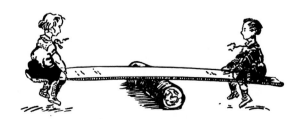

To compare: when we live out of our God-given identity, the negative and positive circumstances that we go through can be used to shape us, not define us. They each have a purpose, but their purpose is not to add to or detract from our personal value; it is to propel us to a hopeful future filled with purpose.

PRETENDING & PERFORMING

One of the great dangers of creating our identities out of culturally valued criteria is that it may not always align with who we truly are. When we adopt something into our lives that falls outside of who we are, it forces us to pretend and perform.

Think of an actor.

They are asked to play a role, and so they dedicate time and attention, costumes and sometimes even body changes to fit the role.

Similarly, when we form an identity that doesn't quite fit with who we are, we too dedicate time and attention to altering ourselves in such a way that will enable us to fit the role. It's like a continual movie set; we wear masks, play roles, act the part, cover up and hustle.

1.   What sort of things do you find yourself doing to act the part and/or to win approval?

It's a little like this: you believe who you are is not enough, therefore you must perform and pretend in order to win value; and you must keep performing and pretending or you'll lose your value.

It can be exhausting, soul-sucking and depriving. We gear ourselves up for another performance. Act good; hide the bad. Sure enough, over time, our identity becomes work.

Do you remember when you were younger and you lied about something to your parents? Do you remember how much work it took to keep up with the lie? Not to mention, the immense amount of guilt that weighed on you?

Pretending and performing our identity is hard work that weighs heavy on us.

2.   Is there any area of your life that you feel exhausted from performing or pretending?

Identity | A Soul Journey

When we feel the need to act out our identity, we experience a great deal of exhaustion. We also experience a great deal of loneliness.

We are unable to experience true connection because true connection takes authenticity—being real, letting the masks come off—something we are afraid to express for fear of losing our identity, worth and value.

We think, "If they knew the real me, they wouldn't love me." And thus, keep parts of ourselves hidden.

Instead of our self-created identity giving us freedom, it holds us in bondage, forcing us to keep on our masks and keep pretending

---

Mark 8:34-36 (Suggested version: The Message)
"Calling the crowd to join his disciples, he said, 'Anyone who intends to come with me has to let me lead. You're not in the driver's seat; I am. Don't run from suffering; embrace it. Follow me and I'll show you how.'"

---

day five
PURSUING PERFECTION CAUSE & EFFECT

THE PURSUIT OF PERFECTION

The journey of transformation is at the core of the God-given identity. With that identity, all of our qualities, characteristics, gifts, passions, skills, talents and experiences are imperfect and undergo a process of lifelong transformation which leads us to become more and more the women God created us to be. There is an understanding that we are all a work-in-progress, and we pursue the act of letting God transform us over time. We are constantly asking, "How can I be the best me?" and tempering that with grace and acceptance for ourselves and those around us.

The self-created identity is more about the pursuit of perfection. I want to talk a little about this pursuit.

Have you ever watched crabs in a bucket? I realize it's a funny question, but next time you go to the beach, catch some sand crabs, put them in a bucket, and watch what they do. They will climb all over each other to get to the top.

The pursuit of perfection, the lifelong pathway of our self-created identities, can be likened to crabs in a bucket. When we derive our value from a broken and conditional system, like that of our culture, there are consequences. At the core of the self-created identity is the trapping pursuit of perfection.

Self-created identities cause us to focus solely on getting to the top. Am I better than, worse than? Am I thinner or bigger? Am I more successful or less successful? Am I smarter or dumber? We are constantly jockeying for position.

We aren't content to simply celebrate what we do well and what another woman does well. We think in order to be of value, we must do it all and be the best or we won't matter. Contentment comes from reaching the top and only from reaching the top.

It isn't about how I can become the best me; it's about how I can become better than "her."

Perfection is all about an outward projection. It's constantly asking, "What will others think?" and living in such a way to please, win approval and earn value from others.

It isn't a process of unfolding, growing and accepting. It's black or white, all or nothing, right or wrong living. It's characterized by constantly looking around at others and back at ourselves to judge or compare. Comparison and judgment are the measuring sticks for

Identity | A Soul Journey

our pursuit of perfection. They are systems we've put into place to tell us how we stack up and how valuable we are.

We have little to no acceptance for the mistakes and failures in life, but rather, shame and punishment for our personal shortcomings and the shortcomings of others. When we experience success in life, we puff ourselves up with pride and arrogance, viewing others as below us in terms of value. Jealousy and envy are common feelings when we hear about or see the success of someone else.

The pursuit of perfection is vicious, graceless and never-ending.

Perhaps the worst part of the pursuit for perfection is that it's a facade. It's like the pot of gold at the end of a rainbow. It doesn't exist, yet we grow up being told to chase it. We will never be perfect at anything, let alone perfect at everything, and yet, we will spend our entire lives chasing after perfection with all amounts of gusto.

1. Can you relate to any of these statements? If so, which ones?

2. Is there an area of life where you are particularly inclined to compare yourself with others?

3. Do you find it difficult to celebrate another woman's success?

THE EFFECT OF CHASING PERFECTION

When I was in middle school I had a group of friends over to my house. We were all hanging out in the kitchen trying to decide what to do. One of my friends noticed a fruit bowl on the counter and picked up what looked like a deliciously ripe peach. He bit down, hard, into that peach and let out a yelp that startled us all. We quickly surrounded my friend to see what had happened, and it didn't take long to realize that Ron had grabbed one of my mom's decorative pieces of fruit, thinking it was the real deal. These particular pieces of fruit felt astonishingly similar to a real piece of fruit and even carried some weight to them. Poor Ron was tricked by what looked like a real piece of fruit only to painfully find out that it was, in fact, a fake.

I tell you this story because this is what tends to happen as we chase after culture approved criteria to make up our identity. From the outside we may look the part, but truthfully we are projecting a fake image of who we really are. Not only that, but the fake image we are projecting is like that peach—a hollow shell with no real meat to it.

Chapter 4 | Self-Created Identity

In contrast to our God-given identity leading us to fulfillment and contentment by allowing our outside life to match our inner life, the result of our self-created identities can lead us to a hollow, disconnected, mask-wearing shell.

THE EFFECTS OF THE SHELL

A few months ago I went shopping for a new pair of jeans. I stepped into the legs of one pair and immediately knew they were going to be tight. I jumped and wiggled and pulled those jeans up and over my booty and then sucked in as much as I possibly could to get them buttoned. At first, I loved the look. I thought they looked great! The problem was my discomfort. I could hardly breathe. As most of us do from time to time, I disregarded my discomfort because of the look and bought the jeans.

A few days later I was going out for dinner and thought, "Oh, I'll wear my new jeans!" What then followed was the most uncomfortable night of my life. I couldn't move in the dang things. I was miserable. I came home, hung them up and laughed to myself.

One month later, I returned the jeans.

Any woman knows that putting on a pair of jeans that doesn't fit leads to frustration, discomfort and misery.

This is very similar to how we feel when we put on a self-created identity that doesn't fit. It's frustrating, uncomfortable and ultimately makes us miserable.

4.   Can you pinpoint an area of your life that you might be feeling the misery or discomfort of an ill-fitting identity?

5.   What area of your life do you find yourself unfulfilled, dissatisfied or discontent?

6.   Compare your answers to the above two questions with an area of your life that you feel comfortable in or fits you well. Can you recognize the difference?

THE FRAGMENTED SELF

On the next page is a diagram to show you the way the self-created identity fragments ourselves into many different parts, both projected and hidden. Compare this diagram to the diagram on page 69 for the God-given identity.

Take a look at this diagram depicting the fragmented self-created identity:

 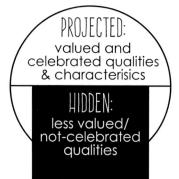 

I don't know if I can be so bold as to say the self-created identity makes it impossible to find our purpose, but I know it at least hinders it. How can we possibly find satisfaction and fulfillment in what we do in life if we can't even find satisfaction and fulfillment in ourselves?

What's more is that the fragmented self also prevents us from having meaningful relationships. If we aren't willing to reveal who we truly are, it will be impossible for anyone to truly get close to us.

The self-created identity, while it's our best attempt at finding ourselves apart from God, leads us down paths of loneliness, discontentment and a fragmented existence.

This is our self-created identity.

Mark 8:37
"What good would it do to get everything you want and lose you, the real you?
What could you ever trade your soul for?"

CHAPTER 5
Processing my Identity

Identity | A Soul Journey

notes

CHAPTER 5 VIDEO SESSION

Process: a series of actions or steps taken in order to achieve a particular end

Most important aspect of processing: God is our processor

A prayer from David: Psalm 139:1-18
- You know everything about me
- You are everywhere
- You made me

David makes a profession of trust in God for 18 verses

Psalm 139:23-24

"Search me, O God, and know my heart; test me and know my anxious thoughts Point out anything in me that offends you, and lead me along the path of everlasting life."

1. David invites God to be the processor
2. David invites God to point out his idols
3. David asks God to lead him along the path of everlasting life

PERSONAL NOTES:

introduction

PROCESSING MY IDENTITY

Have you ever heard of a CPU (Central Processing Unit)? Don't worry; I'm not going to pretend to be an expert on CPUs, or technology for that matter. However, I think a basic understanding of CPUs can offer us some incredible insight on how to move from the first four chapters to this chapter, or rather, how to move from information to action.

The CPU is the key component of a computer system. It contains the circuitry necessary to interpret or execute program instructions. In other words, the CPU is like the brain of a computer. Every instruction, no matter how simple, has to travel through the CPU. Say you type the letter "M" on your keyboard. That information gets sent to the CPU, and the CPU decides what to produce from that typed "M."

In a nutshell, the CPU takes in information, processes it and then spits out action.

We are going to think of this chapter as our CPU.

As of now, we have uncovered how we view ourselves and how we identify ourselves. We have also learned about two different identities we can live out of. What we need to do now is take in all that information and process it together, so that we can determine how we will move forward.

One of the main goals of this chapter is for you to begin to identify the areas of your life that you have been forming a self-created identity out of. A big part of that process will be to understand the roots and origins of those self-created identities (why and how they started). This chapter is set up to help guide you through that process.

This processing is meant to be a joint effort between you and God. A lot of times I quickly brush over a problem so that I can come up with a plan of attack or a quick fix solution. This is an example of me processing on my own.

When we process on our own, we take misguided stabs at what we think we need to improve on or fix. When we process with God, we are guided to the exact places that we need to look deeper into so that God can help heal and transform us into the woman He created us to be.

The intent of this chapter is that you would work through these questions and open yourself up to what God might want to show you or say to you personally.

Think of it like this: In one hand God is holding all of the parts of you that you've uncovered thus far, and in the other hand He's holding all of the information you have learned

Identity | A Soul Journey

thus far. He wants to show you how those two meld together. He wants to show you which parts to take a deeper look at and then what to do with those parts. This is a crucial step in the process of transformation. God wants to help us move away from our self-created identities, and step confidently into our God-given identity. In order to do that, we have to process what those self-created identities are and how they started.

I cannot and will not pretend to know what you need in order to move toward transformation. Only God does. That is why this chapter was the hardest for me to write! In fact, I think I prayed the hardest over this chapter because it requires set aside time and space for you to think, mull over and dialogue with God. In large part, this chapter is out of my control and in your and God's control.

I trust and believe God to show up in real ways as you go through this chapter. I also believe in you, to take the necessary time and space to allow God to work.

Next week, you will be guided through the process of surrendering the areas of self-created identities to God. For now, let's pray for God to lead us through this processing stage.

PRAYER

God, I need you. I need you to reveal the parts of me where I have established a self-created identity. I know sometimes I just don't want to see it.
Will you not only show me those self-created identities,
but will you also help me to understand how these identities came to be?
Please give me your insight and wisdom as we process together. Direct me to the exact places you want me to take a deeper look into.
Give me grace and love as I process through.
Remind me that in everything you have a purpose for good. Amen.

day one

LISTENING FOR GOD

SOLITUDE & LISTENING FOR GOD

As mentioned in the introduction, a lot of this chapter is geared toward helping you process with God. For a lot of us, we are unsure how to hear from God. Often times it requires us to still our lives and quiet the distractions around us. Actions that are few and far between in this day and age.

This beginning section will help you prepare for that.

Read 1 Kings 19:12-13:

> *"A hurricane wind ripped through the mountains and shattered the rocks before God, but God wasn't to be found in the wind; after the wind an earthquake, but God wasn't in the earthquake; and after the earthquake fire, but God wasn't in the fire; and after the fire a gentle and quiet whisper. When Elijah heard the quiet voice, he muffled his face with his great cloak, went to the mouth of the cave, and stood there. A quiet voice asked, "So Elijah, now tell me, what are you doing here?"*

Sometimes I am guilty of looking for some miraculous sign from God rather than seeking Him in the quiet and still moments. Frankly, a miraculous sign is a lot easier to identify. It seems more exciting, dramatic and similar to the pace of our everyday culture. Most often, though, we hear God most clearly when we have stilled the distractions around us and carved out time and space to be quiet before Him.

He doesn't rush. He isn't flashy or enticing. He doesn't clamor for our attention.

Rather,

He comes in peace. He speaks in love. He is gentle and humble in heart.

When I worked as a youth pastor we would take students away on retreats. There was always a rule on these trips that you were not allowed to bring your cell phone. Students continually grumbled at this. What was interesting, though, was about a day or two into the trip, students rarely missed their phones, as well as other distractions they left behind (drama at school, etc). They were too busy connecting with one another, having fun and connecting to God.

As we neared the end of each trip, every time without fail, we saw students' lives changed. Their faith grew, they committed their lives to Christ, and change and transformation took place.

Identity | A Soul Journey

It was always a hard task to explain that God was and is no more near at camp than He is in our everyday life. The real difference between camp and home was our attention and focus. Camp offered undivided time, freedom from distractions and countless opportunities to connect with God and other people seeking God. Home offered an overload of distractions, where time was divided among many things and lots of the people alongside of us were not really concerned with connecting to God.

This experience is not just true for students; it's true for all of us.

Our lives are cluttered with to-do lists, appointments, meetings, activities and noise. Rarely are we ever disconnected. Busyness seems to be the pinnacle of life, and attached to it comes a sort of esteemed significance within our culture. The busier our lives are, the more important we feel.

But, just as God wasn't in the wind, earthquake or fire, neither is He in our constant state of distracted living and busyness.

In order to connect with God, we have to have the courage to get away from all the clutter and truly seek to hear his gentle and quiet whisper. This is our first step.

FINDING SOLITUDE

1.   *"So _____, now tell me, what are you doing here?"* - God

Go ahead and write your name in the above blank.

The hope of this chapter is that you would invite God to be with you as you process. This will require that still, quiet solitude that is free of distractions. (If solitude and alone time are your worst nightmare, I want to encourage you to still try it out. It doesn't have to be for long. A good option might be to choose a place like a coffee shop if it helps to simply be around other people while you seek God.)

My husband's mentor is an incredible man who we are convinced has the least amount of distance between he and God, than anyone else we know.

I asked him one day, "Charles, how do you hear from God?"

He responded with such simplicity, "You wait for Him to speak."

He then went on to say, "You can't rush God. God isn't interested in your agenda. You have to come to Him wanting to truly hear what HE has to say and then give Him the time and attention to speak."

Here are a few tips to help us hear from God:
- Go to a place with the least amount of distraction for you (ex: a hike, your room, a coffee shop)
- Leave your phone behind, turn it on airplane mode, or hide it in a drawer
- Start small: 5, 10, 15 minutes (especially if you are more extroverted)
- Begin with honest prayer. Tell God exactly what you are feeling, thinking, desiring:

94

God, I truly want to hear from you and connect with you. I know that my life has so many distractions which makes this hard to do. I'm sorry for that. Will you help me as I seek to place you as my top priority? As I look over these pages, will you highlight a word or phrase or feeling that you want me to look at further? Bring things to mind, or remind me of something as I process through. Amen.

LEARNING GOD'S VOICE

After Jesus is resurrected, He begins appearing to His people. He wants to show them that He was in fact raised from the dead, and in doing so, has beaten sin & death once and for all. We know that Jesus' appearance had changed drastically because not one of Jesus' people recognized him by sight.

In John 20:15, Mary Magdalene is found weeping at the tomb where Jesus was buried. She tells two angels, who were seated where Jesus' body once was, that "they have taken my Lord away, and I don't know where they have put him." She turned around to see a man standing there and Mary assumes him to be the gardener, but in fact it is Jesus. She pleads with him, "Sir, if you have carried him away, tell me where you have put him and I will get him."

Now, for my favorite part...

Jesus said to her, "Mary."

She turned toward him and cried out in Aramaic, "Rabboni!"

Jesus simply spoke her name and this is how Mary knew it was her Jesus. Mary knew him by His voice.

I've never audibly heard the voice of God, but I have experienced God "speaking" to me—sometimes through a friend, a verse, a metaphor, or during a prayer I might feel a nudge. Learning to identify the voice of God is imperative in our walk with Him. We must learn to distinguish His voice from any other voice, and we must also be able to discern what He is saying to us.

Just like in any relationship in life, learning how to distinguish a loved one's voice is strengthened and developed over the course of the relationship. Our ability to hear God's voice and determine what He is saying to us grows over the course of our lives.

If you've been in relationship with God for some time, you may be able to more readily identify God's voice and conclude what He is saying to you. For those of you who have a newer relationship with God, give yourself time and remember your ability to hear God's voice and discern what He is saying will only strengthen and grow over time.

---

1 Kings 19:12-13
"After the earthquake came a fire, but the Lord was not in the fire. And after the fire came a gentle whisper."

Identity | A Soul Journey

day two
CHARACTERISTICS, ROLES & DREAMS

Here are some questions to consider as you begin to process with God:
- What does God want to "say" to me?
- What does God want to show me?
- What areas of my life does God want to heal?
- And, what self-created identities does God want me to identify?

Recap:
1.   In your own words, write out what a God-given identity is:

2.   In your own words write out what a self-created identity is:

UNCOVERING AND UNDERSTANDING OUR SELF-CREATED IDENTITIES

As mentioned before, each of us have areas of our life that we have built a self-created identity out of. One of the main goals of this chapter is to identify those areas.

The other goal of this chapter is to understand why we built part of our identity out of these areas of our life.

Much like the way a cough is a symptom of a cold, our self-created identities are usually the symptom of a greater issue. I believe that true healing and freedom comes by way of attacking the greater issue; the root of our self-created identities.

For each of the sections in this chapter, select the one statement that best describes you, knowing that none of the statements will fully describe you.

If you strongly feel that none of the statements describe you, write in your own description in the blank space and proceed with answering the questions.

QUALITIES & CHARACTERISTICS:
3.   When it comes to my personal qualities and characteristics:
- ◯ I don't really know who I am or what I want: I listen very strongly for others to tell me who I am and what I should want
- ◯ I just become whoever I think I am supposed to be in the moment, my qualities and characteristics are constantly changing

96

Chapter 5 | Processing My identity

○ I know who I am on the inside, but I pretend to be somebody else on the outside

○ I know who I am and I live my life out of those qualities and characteristics

○ I know some of my qualities and characteristics, but I'm confused which ones are true and which ones I created to win approval or value

○ I know who I am and I live my life out of those qualities and characteristics, but I also attach my personal value to them

○ Other:

Answer the questions below based on your response to question #3 above:

a.   Have you always felt this way when it comes to your qualities and characteristics?

• If not, can you pinpoint when and why it changed?

b.   What effect has this had on your job and/or your experiences in employment?

c.   How has this affected your personal view of yourself?

d.   In what whays has this affected the relationships in your life?

4.   Flip back to Page 30, Question #2 and read through the qualities you circled. Are there any that you circled that you don't think are true of you, but you circled because others have labeled you as such? List any of those self-created qualities below.

5.   Are there any qualities and characteristics that you have placed the sum of your being in, or attached personal value to? (Meaning, without such quality, you would be lost, feel less valuable or worthless?)

6.   What about your characteristics do you want to explore further?

97

Identity | A Soul Journey

FAMILY ROLES:

7. The roles we play or played within our family have an effect on us and can be the birthplace of some aspect(s) of our self-created identity. Look at the list of roles and effects down below. Do any resonate with you?

    ○ role: the achiever — effect: never feels good enough
    ○ role: the rebel — effect: feels left out of the family
    ○ role: the shy or quiet one — effect: feels forgotten
    ○ role: the happy-go-lucky one — effect: fearful & anxious
    ○ other role: — effect:

    a. Can you pinpoint how this role started? Why did you assume this role?

    b. Have you felt any negative or positive effects from assuming this role?

    c. Are there any untrue statements that you have been believing about yourself as a result of this role?

    d. Are there any true qualities or characteristics about yourself in this role? (For example: the achiever role may be assumed by someone who enjoys to always do her best. This is not a negative quality, but it can be used in a negative way by placing the sum of your being in this quality, thinking you need it in order to be of value.)

    e. Do you place your value as a person in this role in any way?

8. Is there a role in your life that you place a large sum of your being in? For instance, a role that you think you need to play in order to be of value?

    ○ wife   ○ mother   ○ friend   ○ employee
    ○ sister   ○ daughter   ○ caretaker   ○ other

    a. Can you imagine yourself apart from this role?

Chapter 5 | Processing My identity

b.　What do you think you have to do in order to fulfill this role?

- How have these requirements/expectations/responsibilities impacted you?

c.　What is the scariest part of not fulfilling this role?

d.　Do you know why you have placed so much of yourself in this role?

e.　Have you seen any negative effects come from placing so much of yourself in this role?

DREAMS

9.　When it comes to dreams for my life and job:
- ○ I feel confined by the stipulations of money, bills, etc.
- ○ I don't really pursue any of them because I rely heavily on comfort and security in my roles/job
- ○ Fear of failure keeps me from dreaming
- ○ There's too much on my plate to even go there
- ○ I don't really feel passionate about anything
- ○ It feels selfish and fairytale-esque
- ○ I had dreams, but I don't really have them anymore
- ○ I have a dream, but I don't know how to pursue it
- ○ I am pursuing a dream that God has given me
- ○ I think I'm too old to pursue my dreams
- ○ Other:

a.　How long have you felt this way? When and how did you begin feeling this way? ("this way" = the box you checked above)

Identity | A Soul Journey

b.   How has this affected your life today (positive and/or negative)?

c.   Do you feel a sense of apathy, complacency or indifference in your job, life and/or dreams?

d.   What holds you back from dreaming and/or pursuing those dreams?

e.   Is there a dream, vision or passion that you believe God has given you that is lying dormant?

f.   What is one thing you would change about your dreams and/or your pursuit of those dreams?

10.   Reflecting back on today's answers, can you identify any areas that you falsely created or adopted as your identity? (For example: placing the sum of your being or finding your personal sense of value primarily from being a mother, or clinging to the quality of achievement that you possess and making that the focus of your identity and value, or believing the happy-go-lucky role in your family defines you). Record any self-created identity areas that you have identified:

Jeremiah 29:11
"'For I know the plans I have for you,' declares the Lord, 'plans to prosper you and not to harm you, plans to give you hope and a future.'"

day three

PERSONAL VALUE & FAITH

AREAS OF PERSONAL VALUE

1. I find a large sum of my personal value:

    ○ in my body   ○ in my accomplishments & achievements

    ○ in my emotional strength   ○ in my looks

    ○ in leadership   ○ in my ability to take control

    ○ in friends/popularity   ○ in perfection

    ○ in my relationship status   ○ in being crazy/spontaneous/wild

    ○ in men   ○ in women

    ○ in my spirituality   ○ in other:

    a. Can you pinpoin a time when this started? Describe it below.

    b. Do you think this originated out of any unmet need you had or have grow-ing up? If so, describe.

    c. How does this affect your view of yourself?

    d. How has this affected your relationships with others?

    e. How has this affected your relationship with God?

    f. What other behaviors have come from finding your value in this area of life?

Identity | A Soul Journey

g. What are the negative effects of finding your value in this area of life?

h. What are the positive effects of finding your value in this area of life?

i. Can you list out anything that you are held back from as a result of finding your value in this area of life?

i. Do you want to continue finding your value in this area of life?

FAITH & GOD

2. My faith can best be described as:
   - ◯ Hot and cold: Sometimes it's great; other times it seems dormant
   - ◯ Vibrant in times of need and/or crisis: When things aren't going so well, I rely on God and feel closer to him
   - ◯ Detached and distant: I don't feel His presence or recognize His presence in my life
   - ◯ Vibrant and committed: I experience God, engage with spiritual practices and have centered my life around Him
   - ◯ Distrusting: I don't trust God and His control
   - ◯ Pleasing God: I think I need to do good in order to win God's love and approval
   - ◯ Fear-based: I'm afraid of messing up and what God might do to me if I do
   - ◯ On a shelf: It's there if I need Him, and I can choose to pick Him up if I want to
   - ◯ Other:

   a. Reflecting on your faith, what do you want to change?

Chapter 5 | Processing My identity

b.   Is your faith at all similar to the feelings you have toward your parents/ guardian?

c.   What is in between you and God?

d.   Is the status of your faith and/or relationship with God the result of a traumatic or hurtful event relating to God or church?

e.   If so, is there anything you need to process with someone, anything you need to let go of or anyone you need to forgive in order to move forward?

f.   Is there an area of your relationship with God that needs healing?

3.   Reflecting back on today's answers, can you identify any areas that you falsely created or adopted as your identity? (For example: finding your personal sense of value primarily in your body, or attaching your identity to your relationship status, or achievements). Record any self-created identity areas that you have identified:

Jeremiah 29:12
"Then you will call on me and come and pray to me, and I will listen to you.
You will seek me and find me when you seek me with all your heart."

Identity | A Soul Journey

day four

CHILDHOOD

1. My home life and childhood can best be described as:
    ○ Abusive: I experienced emotional abuse, verbal abuse, neglect, physical abuse, family violence, and/or sexual abuse.
    ○ Traumatic: I experienced a disordered physical or behavioral state resulting from severe mental or emotional stress or physical injury.
    ○ Loving: My basic needs were cared for, emotional/mental/physical support was provided, and I felt a vital part of the family.
    ○ Emotionally disconnected: My parents and/or guardian did not provide the emotional support needed to process feelings, emotions and the general navigations of life.
    ○ Based on performance: I felt as though love was earned through achieving and performing; I never felt good enough and had a constant fear of disappointing.
    ○ Chaotic: There was no stability for the emotional or physical needs of life; people were constantly coming and going; it was hard to count on anyone or anyone.
    ○ Absent parent(s): One or both parents/guardians were consistently gone, whether it was physically gone or emotionally gone.
    ○ Divided: Home life was split between spaces, whether due to divorce or arguments within the home.
    ○ Other:

    a. How has your childhood affected the relationships in your life?

    b. How has your childhood affected your view of yourself?

    c. How has your childhood affected your view of God?

    d. Are there any unhealthy habits or behaviors that you currently possess that can be attributed to your childhood?

Chapter 5 | Processing My identity

e.   Is there anyone that you need to forgive as a result of what you experienced in your childhood?

f.   Are there any situations or experiences in your childhood that you need to process through properly and allow God to heal?

3.   Reflecting back on today's answers, can you identify any areas that you falsely created or adopted as your identity? (For example: identifying yourself as the people pleaser because of the chaos at home, or viewing yourself as dirty/rejected because of something that happened to you, or always chasing being good enough). Write any self-created identity areas that you have identified below:

_____

Luke 18:16-17
"People brought babies to Jesus, hoping he might touch them. When the disciples saw it, they shooed them off. Jesus called them back. 'Let these children alone. Don't get between them and me. These children are the kingdom's pride and joy. Mark this: Unless you accept God's kingdom in the simplicity of a child, you'll never get in.'"

_____

ACTION STEP
Do something to care for yourself.

105

Identity | A Soul Journey

day five
EVENTS, EXPERIENCES & CIRCUMSTANCES

1.   When thinking back over the positive experiences in my life I:
   ○ feel grateful and recognize them as part of my story
   ○ take pride in them and see myself as more valuable because of them
   ○ expect them and think I deserve them
   ○ feel guilty for having experienced them
   ○ other:

   a.   Do you associate any part of your personal value to these positive experiences? If so, how?

2.   When thinking back over the negative experiences in my life I:
   ○ tend to drown myself in shame and guilt
   ○ can't seem to even think about it, it's too painful/embarrassing
   ○ feel less valuable as a human being
   ○ recognize that it is part of my story
   ○ I have seen how God has used it for good
   ○ other:

   a.   Do you associate any part of your personal value to these negative experiences? If so, how?

   b.   Are there any people that you blamed for your unhappiness and now can recognize your own part in it, too?

   c.   Is there anyone you need to apologize to, in order to move forward?

   d.   Is there anyone you need to forgive in order to move forward?

106

Chapter 5 | Processing My identity

3. When positive circumstances arise, I tend to:
    ○ Celebrate
    ○ Continue on like nothing really happened
    ○ Become fearful of something bad happening
    ○ Become stressed, anxious or worrisome
    ○ Other:

    a.   Do you know why you respond this way?

    b.   Is your response similar to the way your family responded growing up?

    c.   Has your response affected you in any way?

    d.   Do you want to change how you respond?

          If so, how?

4. When negative circumstances arise, I tend to:
    ○ Stuff it down and try to ignore it
    ○ Table my emotions and become "the strong one"
    ○ Seek out a solution quickly
    ○ Seek and cling to control
    ○ Feel it, process it and remain stuck in the pain
    ○ Feel it, process it, and begin to heal from it
    ○ Other:

    a.   Do you know why you respond this way?

107

Identity | A Soul Journey

b.   Is your response similar to the way your family responded growing up?

c.   What affect has this had on your emotional health?

d.   What affect has this had on your relationships?

e.   Do you want to change how you respond?

5.   Reflecting back on today's answers, can you identify any areas that you falsely created or adopted as your identity? (For example: placing the sum of your being in a mistake that you made, identifying yourself as a screw-up, clinging to the role of being the "strong one," or seeing yourself as less valuable because of something you've done). Write any self-created identity areas that you have identified below:

_____

Isaiah 43:18-19
"Forget the former things; do not dwell on the past.
See, I am doing a new thing! Now it springs up; do you not perceive it?
I am making a way in the wilderness and streams in the wasteland."

_____

Chapter 5 | Processing My identity

A LETTER OF ENCOURAGEMENT
Dear friend,

As you wrap up this week, and prepare for your weekly gathering, I want to remind you of God's grace. No matter what you uncovered in this week's chapter, nothing can separate you from the love of God (Romans 8:38-39). He loves you, and His grace covers over you. Not only that, but He is a God of redemption. Redemption is what brings purpose from our pain, which is exactly what God wants to do in and through you.

You may be tempted to look at all of the pain, trials, hardships and/or mistakes in your life and wonder, "what if..." or "why didn't I just..." Those mind wanderings will lead you no-where. What God wants you to do is to keep your eyes locked on Him as He takes your past and does something new right before you (Isaiah 43:19).

Remember back in Chapter 3 when I listed out a few women whose brokenness was turned into something beautiful by God? Cling to that promise. God promises us that in all things He works for our good. He will work for the good of you. He already has a plan to take your junk and turn it into something beautiful...even if you can't see it right now.

The work you are doing is not minor or insignificant. It is courageous and empowering. It can also be very emotional and exhausting. Make sure you give yourself some extra time and space as you continue to process these discoveries. Sometimes that means just sitting on the couch and being quiet for a while, or going for a walk, or calling up a friend.

Lastly, I want to encourage you to keep journeying, my friend. There is more to come and God has the strength to lead you to it and through it.

I am so proud of you.

love,
brooke

DO THIS
Do something nice for someone in your group.

109

CHAPTER 6
Surrender

notes

CHAPTER 6 VIDEO SESSION

Surrender is a good thing when we surrender to the right thing.

Luke 15:17-24

Luke 15:18 *"I will go back to my Father."*

Luke 15:20 *"So he got up and went to his father."*

The father's response:
- robe: a sign of distinction
- ring: a sign of authority
- sandals: sonship (slaves went barefoot)
- kill the fattened calf: a celebration

Two options for surrender
- surrender our self-created identity to God
- surrender our lives to God

PERSONAL NOTES:

Identity | A Soul Journey

introduction

SURRENDER

Surrender is another one of those churchy words that gets thrown around a lot, but never fully explained.

I was talking with a friend of mine who was recently in a small group where the topic of surrender got brought up. Several women in this particular group were stating that the answer to so many of our problems is surrender. You struggle with anxiety? Just surrender it. You deal with depression? Just surrender it. You don't like yourself? Just surrender it.

As these women continued to rattle off the number of problems that could easily be solved by surrender, one sweet (and most definitely humble) woman in the group asked a simple, yet profound question. She said:

> "I believe in God and I am walking with God, but just how is it that one surrenders? I don't really know what that means in a practical sense. I thought I surrendered something to God years ago, but it keeps coming up. Did I do it wrong?"

Can I get an amen? I can't even tell you how often I have thought this quietly to myself.

Before anyone could provide this woman with another churchy answer, another woman from the group jumped in to respond:

> "You know what? I don't think any of us really know how to surrender. I think we are all figuring it out as we go. And I think you asked a really important question that we could all learn from."

Preach it, girl.

A big part of healing, and thus the work of this chapter, is taking an honest look at our lives.

The truth is, we act like surrender is this easy thing to do and something we should all just know how to do.

Do we raise our hands in the air? Do we wave a white flag? Do we write a letter, say a prayer, write it on a balloon and let it go? Just how is it that one surrenders? Let's discuss.

WHAT IS SURRENDER?
Surrender is defined as ceasing resistance to, or, submitting to authority. One of my

favorite descriptions for surrender is: yielding ourselves to God so that He can lead us to His good and perfect plans for us.

Surrender has a lot to do with giving up my control for God's control.

The problem is, I don't like to cease resistance to, I definitely have a hard time submitting to authority, and control is my middle name. So, let's just say that surrender doesn't come naturally to me.

I would love to say that I am alone in this, but I'm guessing you struggle in some way with ceasing resistance to, submitting to authority and/or giving up control. Am I right?

If you are anything like me, giving up control is perhaps one of the hardest things to do. The truth is, I like to be in control. I like to know the outcome. I like to wrap my fingers tightly around things and make sure that I have a good grip on them. Most often I want to live and respond in a way that gives me the least amount of discomfort, and in my eyes that means I must stay in control.

I don't want anyone telling me what I should do! (Side note: my poor husband, parents and those closest to me. Pray for them.)

To be honest, I'm afraid that if I give control over to God in some area of my life, He's going to ask me to do some really difficult things and a large part of me would rather just avoid that.

Anyone with me?

While surrender is indeed giving up control, I have learned that surrender is actually exchanging pseudo-control for inner-freedom.

Say what? Just sit with me in that for a minute.

I say pseudo-control, because let's be honest, we don't really have control over that much in our life. If God wants to do something with us, He will. Yet, He isn't a forceful God, so He lets us make our feeble attempts at controlling our life--hence the pseudo part.

I say inner-freedom because when we surrender, it's truly an act of inwardly letting go... but, not just letting it go into space. Surrender is letting it go into the very trustworthy, fully capable, and completely powerful hands of God.

It's inviting God into our thoughts, heart and soul and letting Him lead us through each emotion, fear, struggle, worry or anxiety. It's an act of humility, acknowledging that not only do we want God's way, but we trust that God's way is the best way. It's relinquishing our grip on the situation and looking for God and His guidance in and through the situation.

The lie that we tend to believe is that our control will bring us peace. The truth is, it does

113

Identity | A Soul Journey

the exact opposite. Our control heaps piles and piles of burden, stress and worry onto our weary little souls.

We will run ourselves into the ground with worry, anxiety, unrest and fear if we are in control. God, and only God, has the ability to see all and know all. His ways are not our ways and His thoughts are not our thoughts. His desire is not to be some cumbesome ruler over us. Rather, He wants to gently lead us toward freedom, rest for our souls, peace of heart and mind and complete joy. He wants to not only lead us through a situation, but He also has the most healing, productive and freeing way of leading us through that situation and to come out on the other side better. What's our role? Let Him. In order to experience that freedom, rest, peace and joy, we must give up control to Him.

Giving up control isn't simply throwing our hands in the air and hoping for the best. It's a conscious and intentional decision we make. It's choosing to identify the things in our life that we are trying to control and acknowledging them before God. We give up control by telling God that we want Him to oversee these identified areas of our life instead of trying to control them ourselves.

There's also another part of surrender that we rarely talk about, and that is the frequency in which we will need to surrender.

SURRENDER: NOT A ONE-TIME THING

We think in our minds that surrender is a one-time thing and that it will be smooth sailing from that point on. The reality is, if we truly want to be free from our trials and burdens, we have to continually surrender them, sometimes on a day-to-day or even hour-by-hour basis.

Think of it like a wedding versus a marriage. A wedding ceremony is a one-time thing. It is a public declaration and designates the beginning of a new journey. It's a large celebration and a symbolic act. From that point on, though, in order to remain in the marriage, the couple will need to put in effort, take steps and make daily decisions that model a marriage relationship. The real work comes after the wedding ceremony and is an everyday decision.

The same is true for surrender. We may get to the place where we desire for God to be in control of some area(s) of our life. And in this chapter I will encourage you to have a sort of surrender ceremony, where you make an outward declaration of surrender. This is like the wedding ceremony. We must remind ourselves, though, that the work isn't over. In fact, it's just begun. From that point on, we will need to make decisions and take daily steps to continue to recognize God as being in control of these areas of our life.

Even after all these years, I still have to surrender my desire to find my worth and value in my image and weight--sometimes it's a daily act of surrender. I have a friend who surrenders on an hourly basis her desire to escape the pain and stress of life through drugs and alcohol. I have another friend who has been surrendering her desire to seek comfort in food for several years. And I have another friend who suffers from waves of depression

114

and anxiety and has learned that every time she finds herself in one of those waves, she must surrender her control and cling to God's control and guidance.

Surrender is not a one-time thing and it's hard work. It requires effort and discipline on our part. In contrast to the outcome of pseudo-control, the effort and discipline we put into surrender actually leads us to freedom. The amount of work you put into surrender today is the amount of freedom you will experience tomorrow.

PRAYER

God, thank you for the freeing act of surrender. I praise you that you are a God who does not lay heavy or ill-fitting burdens on us, but rather you relieve us from those burdens. Thank you. Lord, you know the things in my life that get in the way of you. I'm learning about those things now and I don't want to carry them around anymore. I don't want these things to weigh me down, or prevent me from moving into a more full and abundant life with you. Give me the courage to be honest about these areas and give me the strength to surrender these destructive areas of my life to you. I also ask for your endurance as I learn how to continually surrender over the course of my life. Amen.

Identity | A Soul Journey

day one

PREPARING TO SURRENDER

The goal for you this week is to thoughtfully and authentically get to a place of surrender before God. As mentioned in the introduction to this chapter, surrender is not an easy thing to do. I'm guessing that for most of us, it will be something we need to think over and prepare ourselves for so that we can honestly surrender areas of our life to God. I want to encourage you to take the time you need to get to a place of surrender so that you will be ready to surrender these areas of your life when you gather together with your group.

I also want to give the disclaimer that if you are not ready to surrender, that is okay. I would hate for any of you to simply go through the motions for the sake of completing the chapter. If you need more time, then take it. But, process through why you need more time and share that with your group at your weekly gathering. I'm also going to encourage you to come back to this chapter when you are ready to surrender, whether that is weeks, months or even years from now.

PREPARE TO SURRENDER

We can't get to the practical steps of applying our God-given identity without first addressing the things that get in the way. Glance back through the answers you filled out for chapter five. Give yourself plenty of time to read through your responses, ponder them and then answer the questions below.

1.   What are the things that get in the way of you living out a full, abundant, God-given identity? Write them below. (For example: finding value in achievements, stuck in a painful experience of the past, placing the sum of my being solely in my role as a mother, lack of healing from loss/pain/addiction, looking for value in my body, bitterness and resentment toward someone, fear of the unknown, desire for comfort and security, etc.)

2.   I have placed the sum of my being falsely in these areas:

3.   Write down any areas of your life that you have been trying to control, and instead want God to control:

116

Chapter 6 | Surrender

4. Write down any areas of your life, pursuits, mindsets, beliefs, circumstances, feelings, emotions, trials/hardships, ways of living that you want to surrender:

5. Write down anyone (including yourself) you need to forgive in order to move forward:

6. Write down any hurts that you need healing from in order to move forward:

Matthew 11:28-30
"Come to me, all you who are weary and burdened, and I will give you rest. Take my yoke upon you and learn from me, for I am gentle and humble in heart, and you will find rest for your souls. For my yoke is easy and my burden is light."

Identity | A Soul Journey

day two
PROCESSING SURRENDER

PROCESS THE ACT OF SURRENDER

1. What are you afraid of when it comes to surrendering these areas of your life to God?

2. Is there anything keeping you from wanting to surrender? If so, what?

3. In what specific ways are these areas of life holding you back?

4. In what specific ways do you want freedom?

5. In what ways will surrendering these things to God benefit you?

Galatians 5:1
"Christ has set us free to live a free life. So take your stand!
Never again let anyone put a harness of slavery on you."

DO THIS
Call, text or email someone from your group and ask how you can pray for them.

Identity | A Soul Journey

day three

REPENTANCE, FORGIVENESS & HEALING

The reality is, if we have found our identity in something or someone other than God, we have gone astray; we have sinned. God asks us to love Him with all of our heart, soul, mind and strength, and to have no idols above Him. When we seek our value in anything outside of God, when we identify ourselves by anything not of God, we have sinned.

I understand that the mention of "sin" makes some of us cringe. It feels legalistic and law-based. Sin has been directly correlated with words like hell, fire, and brimstone, and has been used as a fear tactic over the years to cheaply wrangle people into the "salvation pin". If we can set aside all of our preconceived feelings about sin for a minute, I think there is something powerful awaiting us.

Not one person is exempt, or ever will be completely exempt from sin while here on this earth. We all sin and sin does have an effect—it forever separates us from God. But, there is a solution to this separation, and that solution is Jesus. The great news is that our sin has already been covered and paid for by Jesus, it's just there waiting for us to claim it.

As uncomfortable as it may be to acknowledge, it is our sin that required Jesus' death. When we sin, we separate ourselves from God, because God is perfect. We are not able to reconnect ourselves with God. The amazing news of grace is that Jesus' death and resurrection can. Jesus paid for every single sin we will ever commit in our lifetime, and provides the pathway back to reconnection with God. Reconnection to God is a free gift for anyone and everyone. You don't need to jump through any hoops to get it, you don't need to live a perfect life to receive it. You just tell God that you want it and you accept it. In doing so, you are welcomed into the Kingdom of God and given eternal salvation. Yep, it's really that simple.

> If you have not received Jesus' gift of salvation and have not claimed Him as your Savior, turn to page 156 & 157.

While most of us know that Jesus paid for our sins and we have been given forgiveness, often times we take it for granted and fall into the rut of mindlessly expecting forgiveness. It's almost like this secret process happens that we forget to even acknowledge: we sin, God forgives, life moves on. We forget the important step of confessing our sins to God and asking for His forgiveness.

Let me be clear, your salvation and the forgiveness of your sins is not riding on whether or not you confess each and every sin to God. Rather, there is a good gift that we miss out on when we bypass the step of confessing our sins and asking for God's forgiveness.

120

Chapter 6 | Surrender

It isn't meant to shame us, in fact it's meant for the opposite; to free us from guilt. In Psalm 32, verses 1 to 5, David talks about the effects of withholding our confession of sins, and the sweet relief that comes from acknowledging our sins before God. Take a read:

> *"Oh what joy for those*
> *whose disobedience is forgiven,*
> *whose sin is put out of sight!*
> *Yes, what joy for those*
> *whose record the Lord has cleared of guilt,*
> *whose lives are lived in complete honesty!*
> *When I refused to confess my sin,*
> *my body wasted away,*
> *and I groaned all day long.*
> *Day and night your hand of discipline was heavy on me.*
> *My strength evaporated like water in the summer heat.*
>
> *Finally, I confessed all my sins to you*
> *and stopped trying to hide my guilt,*
> *I said to myself, 'I will confess my rebellion to the Lord.'*
> *And you forgave me! All my guilt is gone."*

As part of the surrender process, we are going to pause and actually walk out this very important step; the confession of sins and the asking for forgiveness.

CONFESSION OF SINS

1. Below is an image of the Cross. Think through the ways you have turned your back on God—perhaps in seeking value from your achievements, turning to drugs and/or alcohol to cope with pain, idolizing people's opinions of you over God's—and then write those sins on, around, or hanging from the Cross. This is an act of confessing our sins before God.

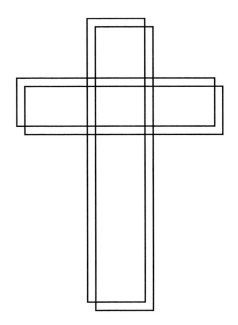

121

Identity | A Soul Journey

ASKING FOR FORGIVENESS

2.   Now, in your own words, write out a letter to God telling Him you are sorry for the ways in which you have turned your back on Him and ask for His forgiveness. It can be short, long, detailed, or concise. Whatever you want to say to God, use this space to do so.

Chapter 6 | Surrender

LAYING YOUR PAINS AT THE FEET OF JESUS

Separate from the ways we have sinned and turned our backs on God, there are also hurts, wounds and pain, that are weighing heavy on us and holding us back from true surrender.

Over and over again we see people fall down at Jesus' feet in brokenness. It is here, at Jesus' feet, that so many people pour out their pain and misery and ask Jesus for healing.

- A man named Jairus came and fell at Jesus' feet, pleading with him to come to his house, because his only daughter was dying in Luke 8:41-42.
- A demon possessed man in Mark 5:1-20 falls at Jesus' feet.
- After a group of lepers were healed, one came back and threw himself at Jesus' feet and thanked Him in Luke 17:11-19.
- Mary, sister to Martha and Lazarus, falls at Jesus' feet after her brother dies in John 11:32.
- A woman who was healed of her internal bleeding by touching Jesus' cloak, falls at his feet in Luke 8:47.

I'm not sure if there are any places of brokenness and pain within you, dear sister, but if there is, we have a Jesus who cries with us, mourns with us, and wants to provide healing comfort to us. Would you take the invitation today to fall at his feet and lay your brokenness down?

"The sacrifices of God are a broken spirit; a broken and contrite heart, O God, you will not despise." Psalm 51:7

3. Below is a picture of what we are going to imagine as being the feet of Jesus. Think through any pains that need healing—loss, divorce, marital crisis, abuse—and write them down below as an act of asking Jesus for healing.

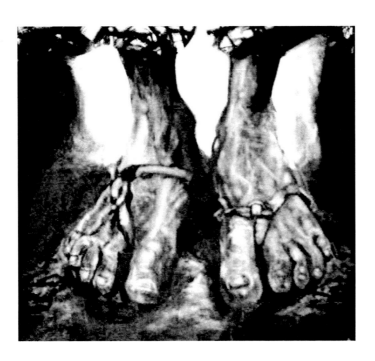

Identity | A Soul Journey

4. After you have written out your brokenness, pain and heartache, feel free to get down on your knees, open your hands—palms facing upwards, and ask Jesus for healing in these specific areas of your life.

Psalm 32:1-5
"Blessed is the one whose transgressions are forgiven, whose sins are covered.
Blessed is the one whose sin the Lord does not count against them
and in whose spirit is no deceit. When I kept silent, my bones wasted away through
my groaning all day long. For day and night your hand was heavy on me;
my strength was sapped as in the heat of summer. Then I acknowledged my sin to
you and did not cover up my iniquity. I said, 'I will confess my transgressions to the
Lord.' And you forgave the guilt of my sin."

Chapter 6 | Surrender

day four

FORGIVENESS OF SELF

For some of you, your inability to forgive yourself for the mistakes you have made is what's holding you back from a full and abundant life with Christ. If you find yourself drowning in shame, viewing yourself as a bad person, or have other feelings similar to these, you may want to consider walking through the process of forgiving yourself.

As mentioned before, I lost my sister in 2011 to a drug overdose. While we weren't completely sure about where my sister was at with the whole God thing, we later learned that she had a deep, and grace-filled connection to God and her Savior, Jesus. Praise God. One day while going through some of her things, my mom found a forgiveness letter that she had written to herself. This letter has, without a doubt, changed my life and walk with God in more ways than one. In this simple letter, my sister taught me the importance of forgiving myself for the mistakes I've made, and how forgiveness for ourselves is what will keep us from drowning in guilt and shame and continuing the cycle of destruction.

For some of us we punish ourselves, or think we need to spend our life paying back for the wrongs we have committed. Although forgiving ourselves is not directly addressed in the Bible, God's forgiveness of us is. We are told that everyone who believes in Jesus Christ is forgiven. If the God of this universe, who has never done anything wrong, has forgiven you, why is it that you think you are justified in withholding forgiveness of yourself? No amount of punishment, shame or guilt will cover up your mistake, only God's grace and forgiveness will.

We have absolutely nothing to gain by withholding forgiveness from ourselves—it will not accomplish any good. We do, however, have life and freedom and joy to gain in releasing our unforgiveness to God.

1.   On the following page is the letter my sister wrote to herself. There are blanks for you to fill in so that you can make this letter personal to you.

125

Identity | A Soul Journey

FORGIVENESS LETTER TO YOURSELF

Dear _____(Your Name),

In order to get back on track and gain some recovery again you need to do a very diffi-cult thing, you need to forgive yourself. I know right now that's the last thing you think you should be doing but if you don't the guilt and shame will just take you down.

Say these words out loud and repeat after me, "I forgive myself for_____

_____

_____."

You're not a bad person, you're an imperfect person and you just forgot to use the tools you have learned.

You're getting another chance by the grace of God, so grab on with both hands and take it. He has a great life planned for you, so live for His will and not yours. You can do it, I believe in you.

Love Always,

_____ (Your Name)

Romans 8:1-4
"Therefore, there is now no condemnation for those who are in Christ Jesus, because through Christ Jesus the law of the Spirit who gives life has set you free from the law of sin and death. For what the law was powerless to do because it was weakened by the flesh, God did by sending his own Son in the likeness of sinful flesh to be a sin offering. And so he condemned sin in the flesh, in order that the righteous require-ment of the law might be fully met in us, who do not live according to the flesh but according to the Spirit."

---

day five

DECISION

At your weekly gathering you will be participating in some sort of "surrender ceremony," with your group. Before going to your gathering, spend some time thinking over this chapter. Flip back through the pages and take in the places of your life that you need to surrender. When you are ready, you can fill out the simple invitation below.

ARE YOU READY TO SURRENDER?

1.   Place an "X" next to the appropriate action below.

Dear God,

I am: _____ **ready** _____ **not ready** to surrender.

Love,

_____

Mark 8:35
"For whoever wants to save their life will lose it, but whoever loses their life for me and for the gospel will save it."

ACTION STEP

Every time you are tempted, pick up a slip of paper, write out what you need to surrender, drop it in a jar. Keep doing that anytime you are tempted.

CHAPTER 7
Apply & Practice the God-Given Identity

notes

CHAPTER 7 VIDEO SESSION

Blueprint for tonight:
- read some words from a guy who hated Christians and then became a Christian
- hear the life story of a woman named Tina
- and talk about something only God can do

Saul is given the new name Paul
- Paulus was the very first person Saul led to a relationship with Jesus
- Saul, renamed Paul, went on to become one of the greatest missionary evangelists of all time

Ephesians 4:22-24
"that, in reference to your former manner of life, you lay aside the old self, which is being corrupted in accordance with the lusts of deceit, and that you be renewed in the spirit of your mind, and put on the new self, which in the likeness of God has been created in righteousness and holiness of the truth."

Put off the old self, put on the new self - referencing the act of changing into clothes
- daily
- temptation
- likeness

Nothing is ever wasted with God

PERSONAL NOTES:

introduction
APPLY & PRACTICE THE GOD-GIVEN IDENTITY

In chapter two, we uncovered our current life. In chapter three we learned about the God-given identity and in chapter four we learned about the self-created identity. In chapter five we processed the life we are currently living and took a deeper look at the things that get in the way of us living out of our God-given identity. In chapter six, we processed and practiced surrender to God.

This chapter is all about applying and practicing our God-given identity.

HOW & WHAT TO APPLY & PRACTICE

Jesus tells us in John 10:10 that He has come so that we may *"have life and have it to the full."*

For most of us, this is our reality:

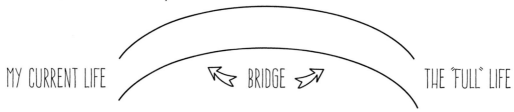

The question most of us are asking is: How do I get across the bridge to the full life?

There are a number of us that believe we can earn our way across the bridge by improving our spiritual practices, such as reading the Bible more, waking up an hour earlier to have more quiet time, going to church every Sunday or praying more often.

I hate to break it to you, but aimlessly adding spiritual practices to your life without any real intention won't get you across the bridge. The full life doesn't come by way of achievement.

Others have thought if they could just muster up enough willpower, surely that would propel them across the bridge.

I'm sorry, my dear, willpower won't get you across either.

The truth is, you alone do not posses the ability to cross the bridge.

Crossing the bridge (AKA changing your life from how you are living now to how you

Chapter 7 | Apply & Practice the God-Given identity

want to live) is accomplished by combining your actions with the power of the Holy Spirit.

Commentary on the verse Romans 1:7 says this:

> *"All Christians are experientially being made increasingly holy by the Holy Spirit."*
> (NIV Study Bible)

It is through experiences (practices) initiated and led by the Holy Spirit that we will begin to change.

> *"Now with the Lord is the Spirit, and where the Spirit of the Lord is there is freedom. And we, who with unveiled faces all reflect the Lord's glory, are being transformed into his likeness with ever increasing glory, which comes from the Lord, who is the Spirit."* 2 Corinthians 3:17-18

Our transformation (metamorphoo) into the likeness of God comes from the Holy Spirit. With that being said, we still have responsibility. It is our job to show up and engage in certain practices, and God will infuse us with the power to make those practices, truth and transformation stick.

What gets you across the bridge is teamwork between you and God.

The hope of this chapter is to give you tangible practices that you can begin applying to your life right now and to help you do those practices with the power and presence of God.

We have broken down identity into these general categories throughout the workbook:
Qualities, Characteristics, Dreams & Passions
Skills, Interests & Gifts
Faith & God
Negative/Positive Experiences & Childhood
Purpose

In chapters five and six you uncovered at least one area of your life that holds you back from living out of your God-given identity. That area of life falls somewhere in one of these categories.

For each of these categories, we have listed out a number of practices to help you apply your God-given identity.

As mentioned throughout this workbook, knowing truth is only half the battle. The other half is living out that truth. I want every single woman holding this workbook to live as the woman God created her to be. That takes practice and intentionality; it takes the tools provided in this chapter and committing to use those tools as you journey toward transformation.

On the pages that follow you will find a wide array of opportunities to practice living as the woman God made you to be. Some of the practices will be reparative, while others

131

will be completely new. All of them are meant to help you take something you know in your head and bring it to color through actions in your life.

> *"Now to Him, who is able to do immeasurably more than all we ask or imagine, according to His power that is at work within us."* Ephesians 3:20

By His power working within us and through us, we will begin to cross that bridge and experience the full life more and more.

UNIQUE PRACTICES

Since uniqueness is of such importance to God, we can expect that our growth and change will come from experiences that are also unique and fit us individually. The following pages reflect that.

What helps your small group leader transform and grow, may not help you. This is extremely important to remember as we apply certain practices to our lives. Comparison will be a likely temptation. Remember, we were each made uniquely, therefore our transformation and means to transformation will also be unique. So, as you read through the following pages, think about what works for you, not anyone else. Ask God what He is wanting you to practice.

THE LAYOUT

Think of this chapter like shopping. Browse through the various practices and pull from the shelf the ones that jump out to you. Only you truly know what areas of your life need practice. If you try out one practice all week, that's great. If you try out a new practice every day, that's great, too. Do what is best for you and your journey.

You are responsible for pursuing transformation, so do what you need to do in order to move toward transformation.

PRAYER

God, I am excited and a little nervous about change. I know that I want the full life that you have promised to us. I also know that I will need your help as I try out some of these practices. Will you give me courage to do them, commitment to stick to them, and power to change the troublesome areas of my life? Show me and lead me to the practices that will help me transform more into the woman you created me to be. Amen.

Chapter 7 | Apply & Practice the God-Given identity

day one
QUALITIES, CHARACTERISTICS, DREAMS, PASSIONS

Just a reminder: these practices will simply be another to-do if you do not invite God to lead you, be with you, and guide you. Remember, it is God's power at work within us that leads to transformation, not how perfectly we complete a practice. Keeping your focus on God as you navigate through this week's content will help with this.

QUALITIES & CHARACTERISTICS

Do you know who you really are? These practices below will help you uncover your true self—unique qualities, personality type, characteristics, and more.

Having a better understanding of who you are and how you are wired is essential to transformation. There are also a few things to be cautious of as you go about the self-discovery process.

- Your results aren't complete truth. These tests are meant to give you a better understanding of yourself, not to define you completely.

- They don't excuse or justify our negative actions and responses. Be wary of taking on the "that's just how I am," attitude.

1.   Take the Myers-Briggs Test (Online)

The Myers-Briggs test is a questionnaire designed to help identify how a person perceives the world and makes decisions. This test is perhaps one of the most powerful tools for understanding your inner-wiring. The test results will give you a 4-letter combination. Each letter signifies a different style.

2.   Take the Enneagram Test (Online)

The Enneagram is a personality test that defines nine interconnected personality types.

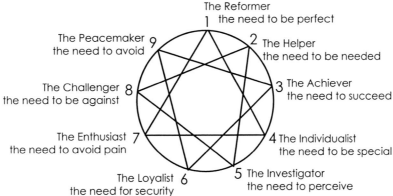

133

Identity | A Soul Journey

There is a book titled "The Enneagram, A Christian Perspective" by Richard Rohr and Andreas Ebert that gives an exhaustive description of the different personality types from the Christian viewpoint. This is by far one of the most underrated personality tests and this book really helps unpack your results.

3.   Identify your qualities as a child

        While this isn't always true, sometimes our purest form of self can be found by studying who we were as a child. Ask a parent or sibling, that watched you grow up, the following questions:

            What sort of things did I enjoy as a child?

            What qualities and characteristics did I display when I was younger?

            Was I involved in any activities or clubs?

            What did I spend my time doing?

            What five words would you use to describe me as a child?

DISCOVERING WHAT GIVES YOU JOY

"To find in ourselves what makes life worth living is risky business, for it means that once we know, we must seek it. A few brave souls do look within and are so moved by what they find that they sacrifice, from then on, whatever is necessary to bring that self into being."
- Marsha Sinetar

4.   Look back to Page 33, Questions 8-10. List out any activities that make you feel excited, enthusiastic and most alive:
        (Ex: making crafts, meeting with someone for coffee, decorating, taking pictures, writing, teaching others, learning, watching movies, listening to music, creating something, serving others, singing, acting, etc.)

        ◯   Are you making regular time for these activities in your life?

                        YES   NO

                If no, how can you make time for these activities?

                ____prioritize and rearrange my schedule
                ____say no to something I'm doing that is draining me
                ____balance my have-to's with my want-to's
                ____other:

134

Chapter 7 | Apply & Practice the God-Given identity

○ Write down one thing that gives you joy that you are going to add to your life:

- Now, take the steps you need to take in order to add that joy into your life (i.e. make an appointment, research, add it into your calendar, remove something from your schedule, etc.)

The things that give us the most joy, satisfaction and fulfillment are confirmation of the unique characteristics God has placed within us. (By the way, I'm not talking about temporary satisfaction or pleasure; I'm talking about deep-down soul satisfaction.)

Sometimes we can over-spiritualize things and think only the churchy examples are from God, like serving the poor, praying or reading the Bible. Some of the greatest freedom I found was when I realized that I experience joy when I decorate my home. It doesn't serve some mighty purpose. It's main purpose is that it gives me joy. This is something that God has given me; a unique way He has made me. It is of no less importance than any other part of myself. It may serve a different purpose than my other qualities, but it doesn't mean it is any less important.

In the movie, "Chariots of Fire," a story about two Olympic runners, the main character, Eric Liddell says this about running, "I believe God made me for a purpose, but He also made me fast. And when I run I feel His pleasure." Doing things that bring joy to our soul gives God pleasure.

If you experience joy—giddiness, a lightness of heart, soul-pleasure—from running, cooking, decorating your home, doing crafts, going for walks or writing poetry, this is part of how God made you, and it's something God wants you to engage in on a regular basis. It doesn't have to serve some mighty and great purpose for it to be worth doing. Sometimes it can simply be about feeling God's pleasure.

DISCOVERING WHAT MAKES YOU CRY

So often we view tears as a bad thing. Sometimes the things that make us cry or touch our hearts in profound ways are actually passions that God has placed within us. For example, I have a friend who feels (far more than anyone else I know) for people with developmental disabilities. She has a passion to serve and love this community of people in a unique and specific way. I have another friend who was so moved by the genocide in Darfur that she would cry every time she read a news article on that subject. She has a passion for Sudanese refugees displaced by the genocide.

There are things that God has hardwired within us to care about. These are the avenues for which we become the hands and feet of Jesus to our hurting world.

135

Identity | A Soul Journey

5.   Think back over the past several years. List out anything below that touched you, moved you, or impacted you in a profound way. What breaks your heart?:

○   Spend some times researching of talking with someone about ways for you to engage with the things you listed above.

○   Write at least one thing you are going to do to pursue the things you are passionate about here:

PRAYING FOR YOUR DREAMS

6.   Glance back to Page 33, Questions 11 and 12. Now, look at Page 99, Question 9. If there is a dream that you feel has been placed within your heart, write that here:

○   Write out a prayer to God concerning this dream. Tell Him what you most want. Ask for His guidance and leadership on how to pursue this dream. Ask Him to be in control. Ask Him to open doors. Ask Him to provide financially. Ask Him whatever is on your heart.

○   Write this prayer in your phone, send it to yourself in an email, write it out and place it next to your bed. Now, find a time in your schedule to pray regularly over this dream. (Add it in to your calendar if you need help to remember!)

Psalm 37:5
"Commit everything you do to the Lord. Trust him, and he will help you."

Chapter 7 | Apply & Practice the God-Given identity

day two

PERSONAL VALUE

PERSONAL VALUE

1.   Create a Personal Value Power Statement

Creating a "power statement" can help you to redefine where your personal value comes from and it provides you with a powerful response when your personal value is in question.

Fill in the blanks below to complete your power statement:

○   My value does not come from _____. I am valuable no matter _____. My value comes from being a whole, imperfect person.

Recite your power statement any time you feel tempted to find your value in what you do, have or what others say about you.

2.   Identify Your Triggers for False Value

What activity, atmosphere or people trigger you to link your value to a false identity? (For example: if you find your value in your body weight, perhaps the gym, or the act of weighing yourself, are triggers that feed a false sense of personal value. Triggers can include social media, certain people, competitions, shopping, etc.)

○   Fast from these triggers: Start with taking a one-week break from this activity, atmosphere or people. After your week is done take inventory of how you feel.

Did the fast help?

Did the fast improve any of my feelings toward my personal value?

Do I need to continue fasting from this area of my life?

○   Claiming Value: Before engaging with the activity, atmosphere or people listed above, remind yourself of your true value as a whole person. Then, continue to recite this truth throughout. (For example: when I am exercising, I will repeat this statement to myself several times: "My value does not come from my body, my weight, my size or the minutes I spend at the gym. I am valuable no matter my weight.")

137

Identity | A Soul Journey

○ Value Reminder: Set a reminder in your phone or on your calendar to go off just before you find yourself engaging with the activity, atmosphere or people listed above. It will remind you to pray and acknowledge before God where your value comes from and ask for His help.

○ Most often, the places we are falsely seeking our personal value from, are also the places we are most tempted to compare ourselves in. For example, if you tend to seek a false sense of personal value from your achievements, you are likely to compare yourself to others' achievements. Write below the area of life you typically compare yourself most to:

○ Now that you have identified when you are most tempted, try and catch your comparing thoughts and replace them with your personal value power statement.

3. Identify quick fixes for personal value

Often times we have quick-fix solutions to give us a shot of personal value when we feel low. Read through the list below and check any boxes of activities that you engage in as a quick-fix solution to personal value.

○ Posting/liking/browsing   ○ Alcohol/drugs
○ Social Media   ○ Achievement(s)
○ Internet   ○ Romantic Relationships
○ TV/Movies   ○ Putting others down
○ Food   ○ Cutting
○ Shopping   ○ Starving yourself/throwing up
○ Exercise   ○ Other:_____

○ For each box you checked above, write out the situation that causes you to turn to one of these quick-fixes

○ Now, think through and process a healthy response to a lack of feeling personal value for each box you checked above. (Ex: take a bath, go for a walk, call a friend and share how you are feeling)

Chapter 7 | Apply & Practice the God-Given identity

○ Ask a close friend to be your accountability partner. Anytime you feel tempted to turn to a quick fix above, contact your accountability partner first, and talk it out. Explore and discuss why you are tempted to reach for a quick fix.

3. Processing what makes a person valuable
Who do you admire most? Who are your heroes? (This can be anyone!) Next to each name, briefly explain why you admire them. (Reminder: Refrain from the temptation to compare, and instead celebrate these people you admire.)

Name: _____

I admire him/her because: _____

Name: _____

I admire him/her because: _____

○ Do any of the reasons you admire these people come from their looks, possessions or external qualities?

○ What sort of qualities do you admire in others?

○ Do you possess any of those inner qualities you admire in others? If so, which ones?

5. Renewing the mind
So much of our unhealthy behaviors, struggles and issues incubate in the mind. They are fed in the mind, they grow in the mind, and eventually they move out of our minds and into our actions, eventually consuming our entire lives.

In Romans 12:2 it says, *"Do not conform any longer to the pattern of this world, but be transformed by the renewing of your mind."*

Identity | A Soul Journey

One of the greatest battles we will ever fight is the battle for a healthy, pure and godly mind. And you guessed it, it takes work!

If you feel like your mind is hatching all sorts of negative behaviors, you have the ability to turn the lights off on the incubation process.

○ First, record some of your negative thoughts below:

○ Now, for each thought you listed, write out a counter thought of truth—a verse or a word from God that is completely true and concrete. Here are a few verses to get you thinking:

I was made unique/wonderful. Psalm 139:14
I am accepted by God. Romans 15:7
I am a daughter of God. Gal 4:7
I am God's friend. John 15:15
I am God's child. Ephesians 1:5
God loves me. Ephesians 5:1
I am loved by God no matter what. Romans 8:39
I am strong in Christ. Philippians 4:13
I am never alone. God is always with me. Hebrews 13:5
God has given me a spirit of power, love & self-control 2Tim1:7

○ Focus on one of your most recurring negative thoughts. For the next week, try to replace that thought as often as possible with the word of truth you listed next to it.

6. People pleasing
    People pleasing is valuing the opinion of others over the opinion of God.

    Where are my people pleasers and approval addicts at? Oh girl, I am with you. For years, the pleasure someone took in me was like breath to my lungs. I couldn't live without it, and I puffed up with the slightest aroma of it.

    In addition, people pleasing served as my moral compass: If it pleased people it was right; if it didn't please people it was wrong. It would be fair to say that my frantic grasping for approval was found in everything I did, from sports and school to serving and loving others. I was solely reliant on the approval of people.

    In hopes to expose the hidden lies and inch us toward a new way of life, I would like to take a minute and highlight the general birthplace for people pleasing and our clamor for approval.

140

Chapter 7 | Apply & Practice the God-Given identity

Somewhere along the way, whether from our culture, the people in our lives or both, we began to believe that we only had value if _____. This likely came from a deep wound within us, the wound of an unmet need. Some sort of God-given need we were wired with was not being met, and therefore we developed some sort of performance, act or role in an attempt to fill that need.

We believed the lie that being ourselves was not enough, and therefore we had to earn our value. People became our gods and approval became the prize to be won.

○ Take a minute and think through how you might finish the following sentences. You may have to jog your memory back to when you were a child.

I only have value if _____

Who I am is not enough; I need to _____

○ Who are the people you are most often seeking approval from or trying to please?

○ Identify some ways that you attempt to please this or these person(s) and write them below. Start small and try to stop yourself from one of these ways in the next few weeks.

○ Apologize to God. People pleasing and approval addiction are sins. They basically equate to valuing the opinion of others more highly than the opinion of God. It can be difficult to understand these behaviors as sins because they have been so normalized in our society. Take a minute and tell God you are sorry for valuing _____'s opinion of you, higher than His.

○ Before seeing this person again, ask a safe person in your life to pray for you. Ask God for help in dethroning their opinion of you and putting His opinion of you back on the throne.

---

2 Timothy 1:7
"For God has not given us a spirit of fear and timidity,
but of power, love, and self- discipline."

141

Identity | A Soul Journey

day three
SPIRITUAL GIFTS, STRENGTHS & TALENTS

SPIRITUAL GIFTS

1. Record your spiritual gifts from the test you took in chapter three (Page 62):

    Our gifts grow, mature and develop over time. God does not give us gifts in full bloom; we have to use them over and over for them to grow and mature. In 2 Timothy 1:6, Paul reminds Timothy to fan into flame the gifts God has given him. This is exactly what each of us need to do when it comes to our spiritual gifts.

    ○   Based on the results of your spiritual gifts test, are you currently using the gifts you have been given?

    YES   NO

    ○   If no, identify someone you can talk to (a leader at your church, a church staff member, a friend) about ways that you can use your spiritual gifts in a practical way.

STRENGTHS

2. Take the Strengthsfinder test (Online)

3. Interview a Friend
    Identify a person or two that truly know you. If you don't think anyone truly knows you, don't ask anyone at all; just skip this step. If you have someone that truly knows you, ask this person some of these questions:

    What do you see as my strengths?

    When have you seen me doing something for which I was made?

    Do you see anything that holds me back?

    Are there any ways that you think I could use my strengths that I'm not already?

Chapter 7 | Apply & Practice the God-Given identity

TALENTS

4.   Read Matthew 25:14-30

Which person in this parable do you most relate to? The one with five talents, two talents, or one talent? Why?

What do you think this passage of scripture is encouraging you to do with the talents God has given you?

Are you doing that?

If you aren't, what can you change in order to do so?

_____

Matthew 25:14-30

_____

DO THIS

Meet up with someone from your group and talk about one of the practices you tried out.

Identity | A Soul Journey

day four

FAITH & GOD

EXPERIENCING GOD

Experiencing God through spiritual practices are simply activities that we engage in to be made more fully alive by the Holy Spirit—activities like running, journaling, meeting with a friend, worshiping or hiking. There's no magical list of what counts and doesn't count when it comes to experiencing God. It's solely about doing the things that allow you to experience God most.

Gary Thomas says that we all have something called "sacred pathways," ways that we find naturally help us experience the presence of God.

1. Glance back to Chapter Two, Day Five, Question 10. Did you have an answer? If you didn't write an answer or are unsure about the answer you wrote, take some time this week or over the next few weeks to try out some of these activities. Take note on which activities made you feel close to God and circle them below (or write out your own).

    nature   people   worship   learning   serving   causes   alone time

2. Build into your schedule consistent time with God. The more time we spend with God, the richer our relationship is with Him. The richer our relationship is with Him, the more clearly we are able to understand Him, and the more satisfaction and fulfillment we will experience. This can look many different ways; it can be taking a daily walk and focusing on God, reading a daily devotional, spending time in prayer each day, going for a hike, journaling, meeting with people. Uncover where you experience God most and build time for it into your life!

Romans 1:20
"For ever since the world was created, people have seen the earth and sky. Through everything God made, they can clearly see his invisible qualities—his eternal power and divine nature. So they have no excuse for not knowing God."

Chapter 7 | Apply & Practice the God-Given identity

day five
EXPERIENCES, ROLES & CHILDHOOD

EXPERIENCES

1.   Sharing with Safe People

God tells us in James 5:16 to confess our sins to one another. He gives profound reasoning for doing this. It's not to feel guilty or ashamed or even to follow some rule. God tells us to confess our sins to one another *"so that we may be healed."*

Sharing our dark, hidden places in life is actually the pathway to healing.

⚪   Is there something you want to share with a safe person so that you can begin to experience healing and freedom in that area of your life?

YES   NO

⚪   Who is a safe person in your life that you can share with?

⚪   Text, call or email this safe person and set up a time to meet. Explain to them that you would like to share something with them that you have been hiding. It's okay to voice your fears to them (I'm afraid you will judge me or think less of me). Then, share with them.

HEALING

2.   What experience from your childhood caused strife or pain? Write it out below. (Ex: being made fun of for my weight in 5th grade)

What I want you to do now is to journey back to that time and imagine a few scenes. Read through the scenes below and then close your eyes and imagine each one happening:

⚪   Imagine your current self showing up to your younger self right after the pain took place. In your imagination, I want you to comfort your younger self. (Imagine grabbing your hand, or gripping your chin and looking into your younger self's eyes.)

⚪   Tell your younger self some Truth that you wish you knew at the time. (Ex: Hey Brooke, your value is not in your weight. Your value comes from the whole girl that God made you to be...etc.)

145

Identity | A Soul Journey

○ Is there anyone you want to say something to from this scene? Tell your younger self what to say to the person inflicting pain.

○ Is there anyone you need to forgive from this scene? Tell your younger self how to forgive and what to say to the person that needs forgiveness.

FAMILIAL ROLES

Often times when we are expected to play a certain role or labeled into a familial role we tend to derive our value from that role. Part of what the God-given identity says is that we are a human being made up of many parts. Our value comes from being a whole human being, not from a certain role we play or a select few qualities. The confusing truth is, people in your family may approve more or less of you based on a role you play. But, this does not detract or add to your worth and value as a human being. If a familial role has been linked to your personal value, it will be important to begin to rewire your thinking and how you see yourself within your family. It can start as simple as reciting truth to yourself over and over again. Fill in the blank below:

3. I am no more or less valuable based on this role in my family:

_____

○ What unhealthy behaviors have stemmed from this role?

○ What is one thing you can do to stop or reverse the unhealthy behaviors listed above? (Ex: if you always assume the planner role, next time plans are being made, decide now that you are going to ask someone else to plan.)

○ Do you need to have a conversation with any of your family members or friends who have placed you in this role?

YES   NO

• If so, here are some important things to process through and share:

I have discovered that it feels like my value as a person comes from the role of_____ in our family/ relationship.

This is how that has made me feel:

This is how I want things to change in our relationship:

Here is what I need from you:

146

Chapter 7 | Apply & Practice the God-Given identity

UNMET NEEDS

God is our ultimate provider. It can be dangerous if we seek people to meet needs that God is wanting to meet first. However, God uses people in wonderful ways in our life to meet various needs and care for us in various ways. There is a healthy balance of communicating our needs to the people in our lives and trusting God with the outcome of those voiced needs. We must remember that people will let us down and not be able to meet all of our needs, however, it can be extremely healthy and beneficial to voice specific needs within a relationship.

4.   Are there any needs that are going or have gone unmet from your parents?

___encouragement ___affirming my body/looks ___to listen more ___respect
___allow me to vent without coming up with a solution ___rules/guidelines
___telling me I'm beautiful ___teaching basic life skills ___emotional support
___time and interest ___guidance ___other:

○   Glance back at Pge 41, Question 9. Based on your answers, decide if you would like to have a conversation with your parents about these areas of unmet needs.

- Initiate a conversation. Ask your mom, dad or guardian if you can talk with them about something a little serious. Set a time and place.
- Pray over the conversation (and ask others to pray for you).
- Be honest about how this came about. "I've been working through this workbook and I realized that I have a need that I want to voice to you."
- Dialogue about your unmet need(s). "I am wanting more emotional support. When I am going through something tough, I'm not sure what I'm feeling and how to navigate through it. Can we talk about those things?"
- Voice any fears or areas of sensitivity. "I want to share with you emotionally but I don't want you to fix me or make me feel like my emotions are not valid. When I do share can you listen to what I have to say?"
- Come up with a plan or system. "When I am wanting your emotional support, I will ask if we can talk and ask for you to give me some emotional support."

5.   Are there any needs that are going or have gone unmet from your spouse?

___encouragement ___affirming my body/looks ___to listen more ___respect
___allow me to vent without coming up with a solution ___telling me I'm beautiful
___patience ___emotional support ___time and interest ___guidance ___other:

Take action:
- Initiate a conversation.
- Pray over the conversation.
- Be honest about how this came about. - Dialogue about your unmet need(s).
- Voice any fears or areas of sensitivity.

147

Identity | A Soul Journey

6. Take a minute and jot down the significant relationships in your life. Write down any needs that maybe you haven't ever vocalized to that person, but it could help for them to know.

For each relationship you listed above with an unmet or unvocalized need:
- Initiate a conversation.
- Pray over the conversation.
- Be honest about how this came about.
- Dialogue about your unmet need(s).
- Voice any fears or areas of sensitivity.
- Come up with a plan or system.

7. Remember back in chapter one when you wrote out your story? Now, you get to write out your story again, this time incorporating all that you learned about yourself throughout this workbook.

Flip back through the chapters of this workbook and try to capture your whole story on the next page. You can write it in bullet points, model it after the letter I wrote to you in the very front of this workbook or come up with your own style to tell your story. No matter how you tell your story, the main goal is for you to capture your entire being, not just part of you. Be aware of the self-created identities that you uncovered and try to leave those out. Talk about your experiences, circumstances and events, whether positive or negative, in such a way that contributes to your story, but does not add or detract from your personal value.

Example:
○ I grew up in Las Vegas
○ I have struggled with weight and image for most of my life
○ I am a leader
○ I find joy in teaching, decorating, and meeting with friends
○ ...

Chapter 7 | Apply & Practice the God-Given identity

MY STORY:

○ Compare the two stories. What was different about the stories? What did you learn?

○ Pray this prayer over your story:
God, this is my story. Help me to embrace my whole story—the good and not-so-good parts. Remind me that my value does not increase by socially accepted or approved characteristics. Remind me also that my value does not decrease based on mistakes, circumstances or happenings. Remind me, God, that your love is unconditional. Regardless of all of the positive things about me and all of the negative things about me, you love me just the same.

○ Now, write out the words "loved" or "covered by grace" or even a word of your own in large letters across your story that you've just written above.

Philippians 4:19
"And my God will meet all your needs
according to the riches of his glory in Christ Jesus."

CONCLUSION

what now?

CONCLUSION

YOU DID IT!

Congratulations, my friend! You made it to the end of this workbook. High five! Low five! Fist bump & fist pump! I know we don't know each other personally, but I want you to know that I really am so proud of you. Not only that, but I am honored and humbled to have journeyed with you over these past several weeks.

I want you to take a second and flip back through the pages of this workbook. Look at all that you filled out, processed through, and did. Doesn't it give you a sense of accomplishment? I think we can both agree that this workbook has been quite the undertaking, and you did it! Sometimes in our walk with God, or even our overall life, we forget to celebrate the good things. I want you to find some way to celebrate the completion of this workbook; go for a walk, take a bath, read a good book, have a cup of tea, meet up with a friend, jump in a pool, go on a weekend getaway. Whatever it is, do something to signify the end of this workbook and all of the hard work you poured into it.

HEALING

As mentioned in the beginning of this workbook and all throughout this workbook, our life is a journey. So, you better believe that this is not the end of your transforming. There are still places of your life to uncover, process, and surrender, and there will always be a need for you to hear truth and apply certain practices to your life with the power of the Holy Spirit. I do hope that this workbook has given you some tools to apply to your life so that you can continue to walk towards transformation. I also hope that this workbook has provided you with a framework for how we practically journey towards a continually transforming life.

I want to give you some practical next steps you can choose to take. Below are a few suggestions as we wrap up the structured format of this workbook and you continue on in the journey:

MEET AND SHARE

Keep processing the aspects of your life with close and safe people. Some of the things that were uncovered in this workbook may need years to process through and digest. Meet up with friends and continue to share honestly and vulnerably. Talk about what you are learning, voice the questions you have, and share about your hurts, fears, struggles, and secrets. Decide if there is something that you want to be held accountable for in moving forward and share that with a close and safe friend (i.e. have your friend check in and see how you are doing with surrendering your people pleasing, etc.)

CONSIDER COUNSELING

Counseling can be a great way to help you get out of a rut that you may be stuck in. I understand that counseling has somewhat of a negative connotation in our society, but honestly, I think every single person can benefit from seeing a counselor at least once in their lifetime. For me personally, I have seen two different counselors in my life when I encountered seasons that seemed a little too confusing to sort through. I cannot tell you how incredibly helpful counseling has been for me. If you feel stuck, confused, or unsure about how to move forward, you may want to consider meeting with a counselor. Or, if you uncovered something significant through the journey of this workbook that requires special help (abuse, sexual abuse, suicidal thoughts, depression, eating disorder, etc.), do not hesitate to see a counselor. Ask some of your friends for recommendations, or go to your local church and ask a pastor for recommendations.

CONSIDER THE SUGGESTED RESOURCES

On the next page you will see a list of recommended resources. Browse through the list and choose a book to read to further grow in a specific area.

LEAD A GROUP

If this workbook impacted you in a positive way, pass it on! Put together a group of women and lead them through this study. Not only are you serving other women, but you will grow in new ways as you lead women through this journey.

JOIN THE GLAM MOVEMENT

Join our Instagram community for updates, encouragement and Truth (@godlovesallofme). Check us out online: www.godlovesallofme.org. Keep your eyes and ears open for our upcoming GLAM events. Pray for our ministry and the women we encounter!

Lastly, don't stop. Keep journeying, my friend. Let God continue to transform you and lead you to your God-given identity and purpose! There are so many women who are journeying alongside of you and cheering you on!

Conclusion | What Now?

RESOURCES

IDENTITY:

The Me I Want to Be, John Ortberg
The Gift of Being Yourself, David Benner
Clout: Discover and Unleash Your God-Given Influence, Jenni Catron

BODY IMAGE & SELF-CONFIDENCE:

The True Measure of a Woman, Lisa Bevere
Made to Crave, Lysa TerKeurst (Devotional)
What's Eating You, Tammy Nelson (Workbook)

FEMALE STRUGGLES:

Every Young Woman's Battle, Shannon Ethridge
Lies Young Women Believe, Nancy DeMoss & Dannah Gresh
The Best Yes, Lysa TerKeurst

DEVOTIONALS:

Jesus Calling, Sarah Young
Savor, Shauna Niequist
A Guide to Prayer for All Who Seek God, Reuben P. Job
I Am Her, M.H. Clark & Heidi Rodriguez (Journal)

AUTHENTIC & VULNERABLE LIVING:

The Gifts of Imperfection, Brene Brown
Daring Greatly, Brene Brown
Rising Strong, Brene Brown
Scary Close, Donald Miller

GRATITUDE & JOY:

Love Does, Bob Goff
One Thousand Gifts, Ann Voskamp

WORKBOOKS:

Restless, Jennie Allen
Freeway, Mike Foster & Garry Poole

Identity | A Soul Journey

THANK YOU

This workbook is the product of true community. You would not be holding it in your hands today had it not been for the love, support, skills, gifts and talents of so many people. I would like to take a minute and thank those people for all that they gave to help see this dream into reality.

First, I want to thank God. This workbook is an offering to Him. I am so grateful that He would choose me to play a small role in His mighty plans. I am humbled, so grateful and filled with joy at the opportunity He gave me to write this. It drew me closer to Him, caused me to fall more in love with Him, and see Him work and move in new ways. Anything good you have received from this workbook is truly from Him. All glory and praise to you, God!

Second, I want to thank my husband, Nolan. He believed in me and the vision of this workbook long before I even believed in it or believed in myself. He has faithfully worked day in and day out to provide for our family, all while cheering me on. He's brainstormed with me, prayed with me, challenged me, supported me, reminded me, and pointed me back to Jesus time and time again. Nolan, I am so grateful for you. I thank God for you, for so many reasons, but particularly for helping me make this workbook a real thing.

Next, I want to thank my parents, Jim & Shelley Paulson. They have stood on the sidelines cheering me on for so many years. Their cheering has given wind to my sails and encouragement to my soul. I am so grateful for their continued love and support of my crazy, wild dreams, and for their belief in me & God.

I want to thank my sister, Lauren. She has since passed away, but I owe some of my deepest soul realizations to her. My life and ministry will forever be changed for the better because of her.

Next, I want to thank Mikala JvR. Thank you for believing in me, for connecting me to so many incredible women, for giving me opportunity after opportunity to share GLAM with your people, and for doing it all without any need or demand for recognition. The truth is, you've given GLAM wings.

I would like to thank Tiffany Matthews, the editor of this workbook. She spent countless hours going through each page, brainstorming with me, editing, editing some more, and giving structure to the finalization process. She is a patient and gracious soul!

I want to thank Aly Allen for her creative design skills and for spending so much of herself to make the layout of this workbook something we all would enjoy to look at.

I would also like to thank Jeff Dillow for the images used throughout this workbook. (www.jeffdillow.com)

154

Conclusion | What Now?

There were a number of women that went through the workbook to provide feedback. I would like to thank those women who gave of their time, shared their ideas and insight, and in turn made this a better workbook for all of us.

Mikala JvR   Charlotte Carlton   Ginny Drennen
Juice Gerughty   Shelley Paulson   Jayme Wilson
Aly Allen   Jenny Hayse   Susan Wilson

I would also like to thank Existence Church in San Diego. They volunteered to be the guinea pigs for this workbook and provided great feedback, support and encouragement! Thanks for taking a chance on GLAM, I am forever grateful.

Lastly, this workbook was the product of a successful Kickstarter Campaign that was completed in November 2014. I would like to name and thank all 68 donors who gave of their resources to make this happen. I truthfully would not have been able to move forward without their support.

Shelley & Jim Paulson	**The Candy Family**	**David & Krista Birnie**
Juice Gerughty	**Laura Wachtmann**	**Michelle & Karina Roeding**
Susan Wilson	**Gigi Wood**	**Terry & Dave Karlman**
Brenda & Jerry Jenkins	**Robin Gavin**	**Cathy Berggren**
Mimi & Burt McDowell	**Samantha Lee**	**Amy Reichart**
Dana Hayse	**Erin Jenkins**	**Lauren Hodgson**
The Dittmar Family	**The Jensen Family**	**Judy Hobbs**
Don & Deb Beeman	**Joe & Faythe Broussard**	**Luci Belcher**
The Anderson Family	**Jenn Karlman**	**Elizabeth McColloch**
Cooper & Karson	**Bonnie Moe**	**Melissa Crutchfield**
Chelsea Gavin	**Bonnie Walter**	**Elsie Woo**
Amanda Loback	**Jil Gertz**	**Sara Smith**
Maggie & Dave Lee	**Charlotte Carlton**	**Marian Collins**
The Drevno Family	**Lori Allen**	**Darci Wentz**
Noreen Carruthers	**Lisa Lindquist**	**Jennie Fletemeyer**
Leslie King	**Gail Sachanko**	**Jodi Davis-Labadie**
Jessie & Natalie Chan	**Danna Demetre**	**Carol Bellerose**
Kerah & Dan Edelstein	**Cheryl Schaff**	**Shannon Taylor**
Melissa Lorenz	**Michael Knapstad**	**Cathy Babcock**
Diana & Jeff McColloch	**Robin Long**	**Jessica Hastings**
Teri O'Neel	**Jenny Hayse**	**Elizabeth Lewis**
Ally Ley	**Abby Ardis**	**Christina H**
Kimberly & Tim Scott		**Alli Waldron**

Identity | A Soul Journey

RECEIVING CHRIST AS SAVIOR

If you have never received Jesus Christ as your personal Savior, or don't have any idea what that means, you are in the right place! And I have great news for you: you can begin a personal relationship with God right now. It's instantaneous, no paperwork required, no hoops to jump through, no processing fees and no lag in delivery time.

Here is what it means to have a relationship with God:

1.   God loves you and God has a plan for your life.

        "For God so loved the world that he gave his one and only Son, that whoever believes in him shall not perish but have eternal life." John 3:16

        "I have come that they may have life, and have it to the full." John 10:10

2.   We all sin and sin separates us from God because God is perfect and completely without sin.

        "...for all have sinned and fall short of the glory of God." Romans 3:23

        "For the wages of sin is death..." (death = spiritual separation from God) Romans 6:23

3.   Jesus Christ died, was buried and then rose from the dead--this was the payment for our sin.

        "But God demonstrates his own love for us in this: While we were still sinners, Christ died for us." Romans 5:8

        "Christ died for our sins according to the Scriptures, that he was buried, that he was raised on the third day according to the Scriptures, and that he appeared to the Twelve. After that, he appeared to more than five hundred..." 1 Cor 15:3-8

        "Jesus answered, 'I am the way and the truth and the life. No one comes to the Father except through me.'" John 14:6

4.   When we receive Christ as our Savior we can experience God's love and know God's plan for our lives.

        "Yet to all who did receive him, to those who believed in his name, he gave the right to become children of God..." John 1:12

        "For it is by grace you have been saved, through faith—and this is not from yourselves, it is the gift of God." Ephesians 2:8

If you agree with and believe in the truths explained above, you can pray right now to receive Jesus as your personal Savior. The way to "receive Jesus" is by praying the prayer below (or something similar) in faith. Basically, you are telling God: I believe in you, I know I need you and I know that Jesus' death makes it possible to be in relationship with you.

> *Jesus, I need you. Thank you for dying on the cross as payment for my sins. I believe that you died, were buried and then rose again beating sin and death once and for all. I accept you as my Lord and Savior. I give my life to you and ask that you be in control. Amen.*

Congratulations!!! You just made the best decision you will ever make in your entire life. As sincere as I can be through words written in a book, I want you to know that I am so glad that you made this decision.

Here are some next steps for you to take:

- Tell someone! Tell your group leader, another believer, or someone at church.
- If you have questions, meet with someone and ask them. Don't be afraid to voice any doubts, too.
- Get a bible (if you don't have one). Most churches will give you one for free.
- Start reading your Bible. A great way to enter into reading your Bible is to go through a daily devotional. Devotionals will give you a verse each day to read and then explain that verse. Take a look at the resource page and choose a devotional from there. I would suggest Jesus Calling to begin.
- Find a church. Our local church is meant to be like our family. It's a place to get poured into each week, a place for us to serve and use our gifts, a place for us to worship God together, and a place for us to develop community.
- Find and/or stay in community. Our walk with God is not meant to be walked alone. Small groups are a great way to help you stay committed, to provide a safe place for sharing and to help you when you need.
- Stay connected with God. The prayer you prayed to receive Jesus as your Savior isn't magic. Just like any relationship, if you want to experience God, you have to spend time with Him. Spending time with God can be done in a number of ways: praying, journaling, hiking, worshiping, etc.

Identity | A Soul Journey

THE GLAM MINISTRY

GLAM: God Loves All of Me is an organization that exists to bridge the divide between women & with God. We do that in four ways:

QUESTIONS — We ask soul-stirring questions

CONVERSATION — We prompt de-masking conversation

STORY — We share our stories

LIMP — We like the saying, "Never trust a leader without a limp." All GLAM leaders are encouraged to lead with a limp.

www.godlovesallofme.org   @godlovesallofme   glaminformation@gmail.com